BY ROBERT EMMET SHERWOOD

———

THIS IS NEW YORK
THE VIRTUOUS KNIGHT
WATERLOO BRIDGE
THE QUEEN'S HUSBAND
THE ROAD TO ROME

———

CHARLES SCRIBNER'S SONS

THIS IS NEW YORK

THIS IS NEW YORK

A PLAY IN THREE ACTS

BY

ROBERT EMMET SHERWOOD

"New York is all right for a visit —
but I wouldn't live there if you gave
me the place."—OLD SAYING.

NEW YORK
CHARLES SCRIBNER'S SONS
1931

TO
MY WIFE

PREFACE

The conflict between the city of New York and the rest of the United States has assumed at times the proportions of a bloodless civil war. It is true that the few New Yorkers who have been conscious of this conflict have been annoyingly unperturbed by it; but the more aggressive Americans of the West have taken it with intense seriousness. There is genuine religious fervor in the oft-repeated statement that "New York is not America."

The deep resentment, not unmixed with fear, which finds expression in this absurd phrase reached its greatest intensity during the Presidential campaign of 1928, when America, as represented by Herbert Hoover of Iowa and California, achieved overwhelming triumph over New York, in the person of Alfred E. Smith.

Among those who were most vociferous in championing the Hoover cause was that sane and civilized Kansan, William Allen White. Being a gentleman as well as a journalist, Mr. White made no attempt to disguise his admiration for Al Smith's forthright integrity, executive ability and good nature. He did not join in the fantastic chorus of Heflins and Simmonses who promised

Protestantism that a vote for Smith was a vote
for the Pope. He did not help to circulate the
rumor that a tunnel was being dug from the Vati-
can in Rome to the White House in Washington
for the purpose of smuggling in His Holiness together with a large stock of contraband chianti.

At the same time, Mr. White darkly warned the
voters—and I wish I could remember his exact
words*—that victory for the flaunter of the
brown derby would spell defeat for those Puritan ideals which form the very warp and woof of
the fabric of American morality. Smith was
shrewd, Smith was candid, courageous and even
honest; and Smith was a menace of inestimable
potency to the church-going, saloon-hating,
monogamous spirit of America. As protagonist
of the New York idea, Smith stood forth as the
arch-enemy of the old-time religion, the faith of
our forefathers. Having crushed that, he would
substitute for it the slick city religion (infinitely
more dangerous, according to Mr. White, than
Catholicism): the "religion of cynical sophistication," of Jimmy Walker, and H. L. Mencken, and
Harold Ross, and Clarence Darrow, and other
assorted non-Americans. (It is strange and it is
comical that humble, reverent Al Smith should
have been endowed with this satanic significance.
That he was so endowed was partially his own

*Of course I could look them up in the files at the Public
Library, but that would involve more bother than this pref-
ace is worth.

fault: he should never have encouraged the bands to play "The Sidewalks of New York" through Nebraska and Oklahoma.)

Mr. White, aided by Senator William E. Borah (temporarily regular), Charles Evans Hughes, Bishop Cannon, Henry Ford, Big Bill ("America First") Thompson, the Anti-Saloon League, the Methodist Board of Temperance, Prohibition and Public Morals, the Women's Christian Temperance Union, the Ku-Klux-Klan, and other individuals and organizations, admirable and otherwise, as well as by the lovely old myth of Coolidge prosperity, managed to assemble for Hoover and America some twenty-one million votes; while Smith and New York were rebuffed with a mere fifteen million popular votes and a disgraceful minority in the Electoral College. Even New York State chose to align itself on the side of America as against Manhattan Island.

So Hoover became President of the United States (and reaped the whirlwind), and it seemed that God's country had been rendered safe for the old-time religion. However . . .

Two years have passed since the landslide and it is becoming more and more apparent that God's country is anything but safe. The Pope has been kept out, to be sure, but the old-time religion is suffering more than ever from a malignant form of senile dementia. The vicious, poisonous influence of New York was not squelched by the deluge

of Republican votes. Indeed, it has been strength-
ened and heartened to a miraculous extent. It
has spread through the press, the radio, the
movies (which talk the language of Broadway),
the magazines and the chain stores. It has in-
vaded and captured every institution of learning:
State universities, young ladies' seminaries and
even divinity schools. It shrieks from the bill-
boards, the loud-speakers, the motor horns. It
runs rampant at every Saturday night dance in
every country club throughout our bewildered
land. Wherever there is a saxophone, or the echo
of one; wherever there is a riveting machine, or
an argument over contract bridge, or a violation
of the speed laws, or a racket, or a photograph
of Clara Bow, or a bottle of illicit gin—there is
New York.

This sad state of affairs is not attributable to
any fiendishly subtle plot by Wall Street, Broadway and Park Avenue to violate America's tra-
ditional innocence; the denizens of those depraved
highways are generally unaware that innocence in
any form still exists. It is attributable to the ever
more apparent fact that, for good or for evil,
New York is America, and the fervent and sincere
denials of William Allen White, and the more fervent but less sincere protests of others of his
Christian brethren, won't make it otherwise. It
is the American spirit in concentrate form (add
grain alcohol and serve). It has always been so.

It was New York that inaugurated the sovereignty of American big business when it gave the wise and cynical statesman, Alexander Hamilton, to the needy U. S. Treasury; and it was New York that opened the way to the new golden era when it gave another of its sons, the colossus, Al Capone, to the parched Middle West.

In his supremely gratifying book, "New York" (it is gratifying at least to the natives of this beleagured city), the Parisian Paul Morand has written:

"Is New York typical of America? No, declare numerous Americans. They are afraid of New York, and they scornfully add that it is the chief Jewish city in the world, the second Italian city, the third German, the sole capital of Ireland. New York is not America, but it is plain to all beholders that all America would like to be New York (except for a few nice Bostonians, a few high officials in Washington, a few artists who like their Arizona ranches, and a few stars in Los Angeles who prefer to gild their skins in the Pacific sun). The great city is the sole refuge from intolerance, from the Puritan inquisition. Manhattan is the microcosm of the United States. All American life is machinery for sensation—and there is more sensation to be got in one day on Broadway than in all the forty-eight States of the Union put together."

Another observant European, Collinson Owen,

of London, has spoken similarly in his interesting book, "The American Illusion":

"Before I landed in New York many Americans, here and there, had said to me, 'Of course, New York is not American. Remember that. It's not the real America.' . . . But once back in New York (after a tour through most of the States) I realized how utterly this was the metropolis of the whole country. . . . Its magazines go everywhere, standardizing ideas; its slang invades the remotest recesses, standardizing speech; its melodies are in every home, standardizing entertainment; the very thought of Broadway, the Main Street of all America, thrills millions who are scattered far and wide. . . . Broadway stands supreme in the world to-day for the fascination of life as expressed in candle power."

It is small wonder that the vanishing Americans of the agrarian West, appalled by the swelling tide of urban pollution, seeing their own children turning into New Yorkers or imitations thereof, should try to combat the evil with the strongest weapon at their command. That weapon is the vote. New York may possess the bulk of the gold and the flesh pots that go with it, but America has a disproportionate majority in Congress. So divinely equable is the system of representation in our republic that it has taken approximately twelve qualified citizens on Manhattan Island to equal the voting power of one

rural Iowan. Thus, the legislative arm of the
government is used to wield the avenging sword
of righteousness. New York is legally compelled
to conform to Utah's ideas on the tariff, Kan-
sas's ideas on prohibition, Idaho's ideas on foreign relations—and, what's more, to pay a con-
siderable part of the expense involved in putting
these ideas into effect.

In spite of which, the hybrid population of the
sinful metropolis can console itself with the knowledge that, if the House of Representatives and
more particularly the Senate are unrepresenta-
tive of New York, they are equally unrepresen-
tative of the United States (as the President of
the United States would be the first to agree).
What is unfair for one is unfair for all, and there-
fore negligible. Laws are made laboriously in
Washington to be shattered easily in West 49th
Street.

So the good, devout people of the plains must
go on envying, and gnashing their teeth, and
praying that Jehovah has not forgotten just how
he settled the grievous problems of Sodom and
Gomorrah.

The antipathy of the farmer for the city slicker
is no new development. It has existed ever since
the country dweller first realized that the town
dwellers were having a better time of it than he.
But this historic hostility is insufficient to account for the venomous hatred of New York as

distinguished from other congested districts in
our broad country. Why is New York identified
as the source of those vices which are common to
all overgrown cities? No one ever shouts that
Chicago is not America, although there are known
to be certain persons there who drink liquor,
smoke cigarettes, abstain from divine worship, en-
joy the more personal favors of painted women,
and commit other acts which, according to the
rural patriot, are wofully un-American. Yet even
Chicago's self-advertised lawlessness is conceded
to be refreshingly native, like Alabama's lynch-
ings: a stimulating reminder of the rugged old
pioneer days.

New York has achieved a specialized character
which has nothing to do with its size, or its opu-
lence, or its favorable location, or its history. It
is due entirely to Broadway. (Note that both
M. Morand and Mr. Owen dwell on Broadway as
the supreme symptom of New York.) If you
would find that definite being known as the typical
New Yorker, you would not look for him among
the bankers of Wall Street, who are virtually in-
distinguishable from the bankers of Lombard
Street; nor among the débutantes and their es-
corts on Park Avenue; nor behind the last of the
brownstone fronts on Murray Hill; nor in the
hives of the tenements; nor in those vast seas of
gruesome uniformity in Queens or the Bronx; you
would look for him on Broadway, and you would

find him. He is probably someone who was born and brought up far from New York; he may have no ties whatever with Manhattan soil beyond those of opportunism; but he will be more thoroughly of New York than is the most legitimate bearer of the oldest Knickerbocker name.

I urge the student of sociology to attend a representative New York first night, preferably in the Ziegfeld or the Guild theatres, and study closely the specimens that crowd the lobby during the intermission. If he can force his way through the drifts of ermine, the tropical tangle of orchidaceous decorations, and the Guerlain mists, he will discover just why it is that New York is hated, and feared, and envied. He will see the efflorescence at the summit of the main stem which gives to New York its unique identity and its bad name.

Here is a list of "typical New Yorkers," taken from a report by the open-eyed Ward Morehouse of the first night audience at a recent revue:

Irving Berlin, Mayor Walker, Marc Connelly, Greta Nissen, March Lachman, Jesse Lasky, Mrs. Somerset Maugham, Earl Carroll, Luella Gear, Arch Selwyn, Otto H. Kahn, Dorothy Fields, Lew Fields, Roy Howard, Wanda Lyon, Fay Marbe, Arthur Richman, Walter Wanger, Fannie Ward, Frank Crowninshield, Texas Guinan, Martin Beck, Miriam Hopkins, George White, Martin Herman, Anita Loos, John Emerson, Jules Glaenzer, Marjorie Oelrichs, Harold Ross, Lillian Gish, Peter Arno, Thomas Meighan, Mrs. Vincent Astor, Joseph Leblang, Claiborne Foster, Gilbert Miller, Louise Groody, Sam H. Harris, Peggy Hopkins Joyce, Lee Shubert, Evelyn Hoey, Charles B. Dillingham, Paul Block, Vincent Lopez, Gladys Glad and Lyman Brown.

Certainly there are, in this group, individuals who are brilliant, charming and even respectable. But put them all together and you have such a horrible gathering as might have attended a rite at the court of Heliogabalus or a celebration of the Black Mass in Byzantium. Place the author of "The Green Pastures" beside the authoress of "Men, Marriage and Me," and the general manager of Cartier's, Inc., beside the cut-rate ticket king, and you will have a true picture of New York—not the New York, perhaps, of fact, but the vastly more infamous New York of fiction.

This is the New York that everybody knows, and that everybody wants to visit, and where nobody cares to live, and about which this play is written. And I confidently assert that, either from the viewpoint of the South Dakota Krulls or from that of the guests at Harry Glassman's party, it is no exaggeration.

R. E. S.

THIS IS NEW YORK

Presented by Arthur Hopkins at the Providence Opera House, November 17th, and at the Plymouth Theatre, New York, November 28th, 1930, with the following cast:

WAITER........................Bruno Wick
MRS. KRULL....................Virginia Howell
SENATOR HARVEY L. KRULL.......Robert T. Haines
HAUSER........................Sam Wren
EMMA KRULL....................Lois Moran
MR. MURCHARD..................Allen Atwell
JOSEPH GRESHAM, JR.............Geoffrey Kerr
LUCILLE.......................Henrietta Ravenell
PHYLLIS ADRIAN.................Audray Dale
HARRY GLASSMAN................Robert Barrat
JEAN DORAN....................Ruth Hammond
BABE SAVITO...................Murray Alper
SHEILA LAVERY.................Lota Bonner
JUDGE GOHAGAN.................Raymond Bramley
MILT FLIESLER.................William T. Carpenter
PETE..........................Frank Layton
CONWAY........................Thaddeus Clancy
ELEVATOR BOY..................Boris Nicholai
KAVANAUGH.....................Tom Fadden
SZTINECK......................Mark Noble
REPORTER......................Charles A. Richards
CAMERA-MAN....................W. W. Watson

————

Staged by Mr. Hopkins

THIS IS NEW YORK

CAST

WAITER
BUS-BOY
MRS. KRULL
SENATOR HARVEY L. KRULL
HAUSER
MR. MURCHARD
EMMA KRULL
JOSEPH GRESHAM, JR.
LUCILLE
PHYLLIS ADRIAN
HARRY GLASSMAN
JEAN DORAN
BABE SAVITO
SHEILA LAVERY
JUDGE GOHAGAN
MILT FLIESLER
PETE
CONWAY
KAVANAUGH
SZTINECK
ELEVATOR-MAN
REPORTER
CAMERA-MAN
TWO MORE CAMERA-MEN

ACT I: *Sitting room in the Krulls' suite in the Hotel Roosevelt.*
Late afternoon.

ACT II: *Living room in Phyllis Adrian's apartment, Central Park West.*
Later that evening.

ACT III: *Same as Act II.*
Later.

ACT I

THIS IS NEW YORK

ACT I

SCENE: *A sitting room in a modest suite in the Hotel Roosevelt, New York City. On the right are windows. At the back, toward the right, is a bedroom door. Another bedroom door is at the left, downstage. Upstage, left, is another door leading to the small entrance hallway.*

The furnishings are standard: one overstuffed couch, toward the right, with standing lamp by it; one easy chair, one somewhat less easy chair, and two or three small chairs that aren't easy at all. The writing desk with telephone is at the back. Between the two doors at the left is a radio cabinet.

It is about six o'clock in the evening. The month is September and the year is 1930.

A WAITER *and* BUS-BOY *are arranging a dinner table in the centre, fussing with the vast array of covered dishes, coffee pots, etc., which make of "room service" the problem that it is.*

MRS. KRULL *is supervising their operations.*

She is about fifty, dignified, formidable—the wife of a veteran Senator and herself a power of no mean proportions in the D. A. R., the W. C. T. U., the National Federation of Women's Clubs, and Washington Society. She delivers almost every speech with the positive assurance of a 9.2-inch howitzer. She is wearing a dressing gown.

MRS. KRULL (*complaint in her voice*)

I told them I wanted the steak *rare*.

(*The* WAITER *produces the largest covered dish from the hot cabinet and shows its contents to* MRS. KRULL.)

WAITER

It is rare, madame. . . . You will see.

(MRS. KRULL *takes up a fork and, bending forward ever so slightly, gives the steak a poke.*)

MRS. KRULL (*not quite convinced*)

I'm sure it's very nice. And the pie?

WAITER

Oh, yes . . .

MRS. KRULL

What do you mean, "Oh, yes"! Is it cold or is it hot?

WAITER

Hot, madame. As you ordered it. (*He lifts the lid.*) See—it steams.

Mrs. Krull

Well . . . that's all right then.

(*The* Bus-Boy *wheels the hot cabinet out of the door, upstage, left.*)

Waiter

And is that all, madame?

Mrs. Krull

I believe it is.

Waiter

Then if I call back in maybe a half hour?

Mrs. Krull

Yes. I imagine that will do.

Waiter

Thank you, madame. (*He gives one last, loving look at the display of electroplated ware and goes out. . . .* Mrs. Krull *goes to the bedroom door, upstage, right, and opens it.*)

Mrs. Krull

The supper's here, Harvey.

(Senator Krull's *booming voice is heard to reply:* "*Be right out. . . .*" Mrs. Krull *then crosses to the other bedroom door and opens it.*)

Mrs. Krull (*in the doorway*)

Not ready yet? (*The only response is a murmur of some kind from the bathroom.* Mrs. Krull

goes on into the room.) I see that you have to
have your cigarette, even in the bathtub. . . .
Well—if you want to eat supper with your father,
you'd better come on. . . . (*She has returned,
and terminates her own speech by shutting the
door, with some emphasis.*)

(SENATOR KRULL *comes in from the bedroom
at the back. He is a big, imposing man, with a
square face, a New Willard hair-cut, and shoul-
ders that are perfectly designed for the support
of a toga. He is wearing black dress trousers,
with belt; a pleated dress shirt; a turned-down
collar with wide black bow tie; and no coat or
waistcoat. He is groping his way through the ex-
cessive pages of the New York Sun. He goes to
the table and sits down, still turning page after
page of the newspaper, evidently annoyed at his
inability to find what he is looking for.* MRS.
KRULL *sits down opposite him, but she is not par-
taking of the repast.*)

KRULL

You can't find anything in these New York papers. Nothing but New York, New York, New
York—and its filthy rackets. To look at this paper you'd think the rest of the country doesn't
exist—and then they talk about provincialism.
. . . Oh! Here it is—and on page . . . (*he
looks at the top of the page*) . . . page 16! And
only that much. (*He holds his thumb and fore-*

finger about three inches apart to inform his wife.) That much, on page 16, to announce my arrival in this city. That will give you a notion of what New York thinks of South Dakota.

Mrs. Krull

I'm sure South Dakota is very glad indeed to return the compliment. (*She has poured the coffee for him and hands him the cup.*)

Krull (*having read the brief notice*)

Here—want to see what it says? (*He hands her the paper. She reads the item, then lays the paper, neatly folded, on the table. Krull immediately starts to attack the steak, following each hearty mouthful with a gulp of coffee.*) Can you believe it, this steak is actually rare!

Mrs. Krull

I know. I told them. And the pie is nice and warm.

Krull

Where's Emmy?

Mrs. Krull

I just called her. She was taking a bath.

Krull

Taking a bath? I thought she wasn't going out anywhere.

MRS. KRULL

She said she wasn't. But anyway, she *had* to have a bath, and a cigarette while she's at it, too.

KRULL

Well, there's certainly no harm in having cleanly habits. But her supper'll get cold. Emmy! (*There is no response. The telephone rings.*) You better take it. If it's for me, see who it is.

(MRS. KRULL *goes to the telephone.*)

MRS. KRULL

Hello. . . . Yes. . . . Oh, just one moment. Just hold the line. . . . (*To* KRULL.) It's somebody from a newspaper.

KRULL (*not displeased*)

Oh! What paper is it?

MRS. KRULL

What paper do you represent? . . . It's *The Evening Telegram.*

KRULL

The Telegram. . . . Oh, yes—that's one of the Scripps-Howard group. They're all right. . . .

MRS. KRULL

He's downstairs in the lobby.

KRULL

I'll see him.

MRS. KRULL

The Senator says you may come right up.
. . . Yes. . . . (*She hangs up.*) You'd better
have your coat on. I'll get it.

KRULL

Thanks, honey. (*She goes out.* KRULL *sees
The Sun folded so as to show the notice devoted
to the news of his arrival. He carefully refolds
the paper so that the front page is again in front.*
MRS. KRULL *returns with his dinner coat and
waistcoat.*)

MRS. KRULL

I'll finish dressing while you're talking to him.
And don't let him keep you too long, because we'll
have to leave the hotel by seven sharp.

KRULL

I know. (*He is putting his coat and waistcoat
on before a mirror.* MRS. KRULL, *on the way out,
pauses.*)

MRS. KRULL

Harvey . . .

KRULL

Well?

MRS. KRULL

It just happened to occur to me. . . . This
Telegram newspaper isn't one of the filthy scandal sheets, is it?

Krull

I told you it's one of the Scripps-Howard chain, didn't I? They've got papers, *good* papers, in a lot of different cities all over the Middle West. . . .

Mrs. Krull

Well—just be careful to see that he adheres strictly to national affairs in this interview. If he should happen to ask you anything about *her*. . . . (*With a glance toward the left.*)

Krull (*back at the steak*)

I think I can assure you that twenty years of experience have fitted me to hold my own with newspaper men. (*There is a knock from the corridor at the left.*) You go on now and get dressed.

Mrs. Krull

Of course—if you can find *out* anything . . .

Krull

I'll find it out. . . . Come in!

(Mrs. Krull *goes out at the back, as the outer door opens and* Hauser *comes in.* Hauser *is a thin, studious and patently weary reporter, with horn-rimmed glasses and an expression in which are mingled in almost equal proportions discreet deference and wholesome contempt.*)

Hauser

Good evening, Senator. I must apologize for bothering you.

KRULL

That's all right, my friend. Sit down, and fire away—if you don't mind watching me eat my supper. . . . Will you have anything yourself?

HAUSER

Why, thank you, I . . .

KRULL

Cup of coffee, toast . . .? (*He indicates the array of dishes.*)

HAUSER

No, I don't believe so, thanks. . . . But aren't you going to the banquet, Senator?

KRULL

I am. But this is my meal, right here. Confidentially, I always eat a good steak before attending a banquet.

HAUSER

That's a fine idea.

KRULL

I can't speak on an empty stomach. And if you rely on what they give you at these affairs, you go hungry. I mean to say—they stick a dried chicken wing in front of you, and before you have a chance to pick at even that, the waiter sneaks up on you and the next thing you know, the bird has flown. (*He chuckles.*)

HAUSER

Oh, that's very funny.

KRULL

Well, what can I do for you?

HAUSER

Hauser is my name, Senator. I'm from the New York *Evening Telegram*.

KRULL

One of the Scripps-Howard group, isn't it?

HAUSER

Yes, sir—that's right. . . .

KRULL

Roy Howard is a good friend of mine. A very able man.

HAUSER

Yes. How long are you going to be with us in New York, Senator?

KRULL

Briefly, I'm happy to say. We just came up from Washington, stopping over here solely for this banquet to-night. To-morrow morning we go on to Boston to participate in the D. A. R. pilgrimage to the shrines at Lexington and Concord. Mrs. Krull, as you doubtless know, is one of the officers of the D. A. R. After that we're going

home, to South Dakota, to get busy on the campaign.

HAUSER

Is your daughter accompanying you?

KRULL

She is. Did you wish to ask me anything about
my speech to-night?

HAUSER

Oh, no, Senator. We have a copy in the office,
all set up. What I was particularly anxious to
talk to you about was something special, a sort of
unique idea, of our own. We're about to run a
series of feature stories on the question, "Should
New York Secede from the Union?"

KRULL

Oh! (*An exclamation of sarcasm.*)

HAUSER

Yes, Senator. You know what news is these
days. I mean it's scarce, like everything else.

KRULL

And you have to fill your first page somehow,
eh? Am I right about that?

HAUSER

You're entirely right. We're getting statements
on this question from a lot of leading national

figures: Henry Ford, Dr. Nicholas Murray Butler, Ruth Hanna McCormick, Heywood Broun
. . . and we'd like particularly to hear from you.
As a distinguished member of the Senate Foreign
Relations Committee, and with your reputation
for vigorous and highly original opinions, we felt
sure you'd have something telling to say. . . .

KRULL

You want a comment. Very well: (*He wipes
his mouth.*) I'd consider the secession of New
York City to be an unmitigated blessing. (*He
says this with the air of one who is expressing a
"vigorous and highly original opinion."*)

HAUSER

A blessing for New York City?

KRULL

For the United States of America.

HAUSER

May we quote that?

KRULL

You may.

HAUSER

And if the people of New York should take
such action, and form a new, autonomous State,
what do you believe the President would do?

Would he call out the military forces, as Lincoln did in '61, or would he consent to accept the right of the people of this city to withdraw . . .?

KRULL

The President would undoubtedly appoint a commission of inexperienced, ineffectual amateurs to investigate the matter. In other words, the President would have no idea what to do, and would compromise by doing nothing.

HAUSER

May we quote that also?

KRULL

You certainly may. . . . Though not as coming from me.

HAUSER

I see, Senator. Now, in the event of this hypothetical secession, what would be the reaction of the people out West, in your own constituency . . .?

(EMMA KRULL *has come in from the left. She is just under twenty years of age, clean, candid and alluring. She is a great problem to her parents. She is wearing a rather masculine wrapper and apparently nothing else. Her feet are clumping in mules. When she sees* HAUSER, *she pauses momentarily in her advance toward the table.*)

Emma

Oh. (*She is not startled, merely mildly surprised.*)

Krull

You go back to your room.

Emma

I thought dinner was ready.

Krull

I'll send yours in. You go on, now. This gentleman is from the press and we're busy. . . .

Emma

Oh, a newspaper man. Well, in that case, you'll forgive me, won't you? (*She goes to the table and starts lifting lids.*) Which is my soup? (*She finds the soup and starts ladling some out into a plate.*) Is there any toast?

Krull

There it is. . . . Come on now, Emma, you get back to your room.

(Emma *is having difficulty with the plates.*)

Emma (*to* Hauser)

Would you mind helping me with these?

Hauser

Why, not at all. (*She takes the soup plate in both hands. He takes the toast plate and the butter.*)

Emma

Oh—and I forgot the celery.

Hauser

I'll get it.

Emma

Sorry to have interrupted you, Pop. (*She goes out at the left, followed by* Hauser. *Her voice is heard, offstage:* "Put them down .here. . . . Thanks a lot.")

(*The telephone rings.* Krull, *irritated, answers it.*)

Krull

Who is it? . . . Yes. . . . Oh, yes. . . . Yes— come right up. Yes—1247. . . . (*He hangs up.* Hauser *comes back.*) Will you kindly close that door?

(Hauser *does so.*)

Hauser

Charming daughter you have there, Senator.

Krull

Yes, she's well liked.

Hauser

You'll forgive me, Senator, for intruding on your privacy . . . but is there any truth in the report of her engagement to Joseph Gresham, Jr.?

KRULL

Where did you hear any such report as that?

HAUSER

You must know that it's been printed.

KRULL

By some cheap scandal-monger.

HAUSER

Walter Winchell.

KRULL

Do you happen to know him?

HAUSER

I've seen him around.

KRULL

He had no conceivable authority for the statement that my daughter and this young Gresham are—are to be . . .

HAUSER

Sealed.

KRULL

Whatever the vulgarism was. It came as a distinct surprise to Mrs. Krull and me, *and*, I might add, to our daughter. Where did the man get such a notion?

HAUSER

I'm afraid it's a rather obvious one. Your daughter and Mr. Gresham have been friends for some time. At least, the rotogravure sections have been full of . . .

KRULL

There's been too much publicity.

HAUSER

It's inevitable, Senator. They both come from prominent families.

KRULL

My daughter engages in many social activities in Washington and in Virginia. She is a keen horse-woman, and has mingled with a set of people who are disposed in the same way. Young Gresham happens to be one of them. He is an acquaintance of hers—one of many, in fact. That is all.

HAUSER

But Winchell is generally right, Senator.

KRULL

I am expressing no opinion on his veraciousness. I am only telling you that this time he has been misinformed.

HAUSER

I see. . . .

KRULL

What do you know about this young Gresham?

HAUSER

Just what everyone knows. He's the son of Joseph K. Gresham, and the grandson of old Peter Gresham, and . . .

KRULL

What's his reputation around here?

HAUSER

He's recognized as what they call an ardent sportsman—polo, racing, and all the rest. . . . If there's any more specialized information you'd like to have, I might be able to look it up. . . .

KRULL

I hardly think you need bother. . . . (*There is a knock on the door.*) Come in.

(MR. MURCHARD *comes in. He is an earnest fellow, with a Y. M. C. A. manner and faultless evening attire. He talks with extraordinary rapidity.*)

MURCHARD

Senator Krull. (*He gives* KRULL *a manly handclasp.*) I'm George Murchard, secretary of the committee on arrangements for this evening.

KRULL (*heartily*)

Good *evening*, Mr. Murchard!

MURCHARD

The committee has asked me to come and . . .

KRULL (*turning to* HAUSER)

I'm afraid I'll have to call the interview at an end.

HAUSER

Certainly, Senator. (*He gets up.*) It was very good of you to . . .

KRULL

Don't mention it.

HAUSER

I understand that we're running an editorial on your speech in the paper to-morrow afternoon.

KRULL

I won't be here to see it. Good evening.

HAUSER

Good evening.

MURCHARD (*politely*)

Good evening. (HAUSER *has gone.*) Well, Senator, the committee wished me to express to you some measure of our—our gratification that you're to be with us to-night, and to do all in my power to facilitate in any possible way . . .

KRULL

Have a seat.

MURCHARD

Thank you—I'm not going to keep you a moment. . . . Now—we've arranged for a nation-wide hook-up on the Blue Chain, N. B. C.—that'll be handled out in South Dakota from Station KPKH, Sioux Falls. The banquet broadcast will commence at 9 P.M. They've promised to have Louis Bettaver on the mike, so you can rest assured that the announcing will be well taken care of. We're figuring that you'll go on the air shortly before 10 P.M. at the latest. . . .

KRULL

I assume that I will be the last speaker.

MURCHARD

Needless to say, Senator, you're the trump card on our little programme. . . .

KRULL

Who's preceding me?

MURCHARD (*taking out a typewritten sheet*)

I've brought the order with me. . . . Let's see —the first will be Bishop Deckwith, Methodist, of Idaho, who will deliver the invocation. Then we'll have a few remarks from the chairman—our president, Mr. Sorensen, of Spokane, whom you of course know. He will introduce Mr. Myron L. Maxwell of St. Paul, who will speak on the outlook in the Northwest from the investment banker's angle. After him comes . . . the celebrated humorist, Irving S. Cobb—and I think we can count on him for something facetious. (*With a deprecating laugh, expressive of* MR. MURCHARD's *opinion of facetiousness.*) . . . And then Mr. Sorensen will call upon the assemblage to rise to the national anthem, following which you will speak.

KRULL

I think you've got a well-balanced programme there.

MURCHARD (*with another deprecating laugh*)

Well, I can tell you, Senator, our committee has put a lot of thought into it and plenty of good old-fashioned elbow grease, too. Now there's one other little matter. . . . (*He takes from his inside pocket a long envelope and hands it to* KRULL.) Mr. Glosser wanted me to hand you this—thinking it might be—better—to have it out of the way beforehand. (KRULL *seems to be planning to open it, in evident doubt as to its contents.* MURCHARD *has wished to avoid actual mention of sordid subjects, but deems it necessary to explain.*) It's the—check—the little matter of the—fee.

KRULL

Oh—oh, yes. . . . (*He puts the envelope in his pocket.*)

MURCHARD

Now, Senator, if you'll excuse me. I'll be running on over to the hotel. There are a few last-minute loose ends to be gathered up, as you may imagine. By the way, the committee has been pleased to place a private car at the disposal of Mrs. Krull and yourself. It will be waiting downstairs at the 45th Street entrance to take you right over to the Astor, where I will be waiting to meet you. . . .

KRULL

That's very thoughtful.

MURCHARD

And I think we can promise you a really intelligent and appreciative audience—all men and women from our own part of the country and proud of it!

KRULL

It'll be a pleasure, I'm sure.

MURCHARD

Till seven-thirty, then. (*He accompanies this with another manly handclasp and goes out. KRULL goes to the door at the back, opens it, and calls "All right, honey." MRS. KRULL comes out.*)

MRS. KRULL

Well, what did that reporter say?

KRULL

He left. There was another man in here, from the banquet committee. He gave me the check.

MRS. KRULL

That's good. But what about the reporter? Did you find anything out?

KRULL

No—but we were right about what he came for. It was to pump me about Emmy. He started off with some cock-and-bull story about New York seceding, but he soon had the conversation steered around to this miserable rumor. . . .

MRS. KRULL

Did he tell you anything?

KRULL

Oh, he was guarded. But his very reluctance to say anything about Gresham's reputation proves that we have grounds for suspicion.

MRS. KRULL

So far as I'm concerned, we don't need any more information about him. Just to look at him is enough to know what he is.

KRULL

To look at him, and to hear that affected way he talks. I know when this started. It started when she began mixing herself up with that set at the British Embassy—that's when. . . .

MRS. KRULL

We're not concerned now with how it started. What we've got to face is *how* and *when* it is going to end. . . .

KRULL

We've got to go carefully with her. She's a self-willed little thing.

MRS. KRULL

She's got to be made to understand the gravity of it. She must be told, and told *definitely*, what the results would be of any newspaper notoriety.

KRULL

I don't like to threaten her.

MRS. KRULL

Very well, then. If you choose to shirk your responsibilities, then it's up to me. It's always up to me. . . .

KRULL (*thundering, as he crosses to the left*) Have I ever shirked my responsibilities?

MRS. KRULL

You always do—where she's concerned.
(KRULL *opens the door of* EMMA's *bedroom.*)

KRULL

Emma! (EMMA's *voice is heard to reply, "Yes, Pop?"*) Come here!

MRS. KRULL

What are you going to say?

KRULL

You'll see what I'll . . .
(EMMA *comes in, eating a stalk of celery.*)

EMMA

Oh, he's gone. (*She goes to the table and sits down to go on with her meal.*) Isn't it time for you to be leaving?

KRULL

I suppose you know why that reporter came here?

EMMA

Was it something about the tariff?

KRULL

He wanted to talk about you.

EMMA

Me?

KRULL

He tried to get me to confirm the rumor of your engagement.

EMMA

What did you say to him?

Mrs. Krull

What could your father say, when you've persistently refused to take either him or me into your confidence?

Emma

I don't see that it's a matter of any interest to the newspapers.

Krull

Oh, isn't it! It's just the sort of thing the yellow New York press would jump at. This young man's family are well known here, and you aren't without a certain prominence yourself.

Emma

Well, if it makes a good enough story, you certainly ought not to complain, Pop. It may get you back on the front page.

Mrs. Krull

Are you engaged to him, or are you not?

Emma

Before I answer—just who is it you're talking about?

Mrs. Krull

This young Gresham that everyone is mentioning in . . .

Krull

Are you engaged to him?

EMMA

In a way . . . yes.

MRS. KRULL

I knew it!

KRULL

Yes, and so did someone named Winchell. . . .
When did this happen?

EMMA

Last week.

KRULL

Where?

EMMA

Down in Warrenton.

MRS. KRULL

When you were visiting with the Frasers!

EMMA

That was the occasion.

KRULL

I suppose you know all about him?

EMMA

I've been told that his family owns a large part
of Manhattan Island, on account of having got
here early. And one of his horses won the Grand
National last spring. . . .

KRULL

And have you also been told that his conduct has been notoriously bad, here and in Europe?

MRS. KRULL

Or that he was dismissed from Yale for having entertained a young woman in his dormitory . . .?

KRULL

We needn't mention that.

EMMA

He's told me all about that case, Mother. He took her in because she was hungry, and it was snowing outside.

MRS. KRULL

Very charitable, I'm sure. But if you imagine that we covet a son-in-law of that particular stamp, you're very much . . .

EMMA

It's too late, mother. I've practically promised to give him my heart and hand.

KRULL

It's one promise you can break and, by the Eternal, will break, before this evening is out. . . .

MRS. KRULL

Is he here, in New York?

EMMA

Oh, yes. He's here. He ought to be around before very long.

KRULL

You're planning to go out with him?

EMMA

No, no. I thought we could just sit here and listen to your speech over the radio.

MRS. KRULL

Why does he want to marry you?

EMMA

That's something that I've wondered about.

KRULL

You might have done well to have wondered about it a little more acutely. You ought to know that you're not his sort—thank heaven! A girl of your background and upbringing in the Northwest has nothing whatever in common . . .

EMMA

I've lived in the East all the time you've been Senator—and that's been forever.

MRS. KRULL

There are some things that environment can never alter. You come of a fine, sturdy, pioneer stock. He comes of an old, decayed, dissipated . . . Well, I won't say what I think. . . .

EMMA

I swear I don't know what it is that makes him want to marry me. It must be that he wants my body!

MRS. KRULL

Emma!

EMMA

Well, then, mother—don't invite such remarks by asking a lot of impossible questions. Why shouldn't I marry him? He's good-looking, he's strong, he's nice and he certainly is able to provide for me.

MRS. KRULL

And he's capable of making you miserably unhappy—of ruining your whole life.

EMMA

Yes—I suppose that's true enough.

KRULL

I don't like to bring my own affairs into this discussion, Emma. But you may not be aware that there's an election in South Dakota this fall.

EMMA

Oh, come, Pop—you're not worrying about that. You've never lost an election yet.

KRULL

I only got through the Republican primaries by the skin of my teeth. You've got to realize that

the situation this year is a precarious one—
thanks to our estimable friend in the White
House. They're raising all sorts of false issues,
business depression, prohibition, internationalism,
to cloud the main issue.

EMMA

What's that?

KRULL

It's whether the control of our government is
going to be turned over to a pack of gangsters
—well, you wouldn't understand. Anyway—I'm
in for a hard fight.

EMMA

But what has my marriage to Joe Gresham got
to do with it?

MRS. KRULL

It would have just the same effect on the minds
of people out home as if you married a boot-
legger.

EMMA

I don't think I see the connection.

MRS. KRULL

Because you don't quite know what a force the
women's vote is in South Dakota.

KRULL

All the newspapers around here are eager to
discredit me. They hate me and fear me, because
I've stood with men like Brookhart against their

so-called liberalism. And you can be sure that
they'd lovingly exploit all the unsavory details
in young Gresham's past in an effort to embar-
rass me.

EMMA

What if they do? What if Joe has got himself mixed up in a few messes? He was born rich,
and it's taken him a long time to get over it.
Everyone around here knows he's all right—and
that the girl who marries him won't be contami-
nated.

KRULL

Perhaps everyone here knows it. But there's
something you've got to learn, my girl. And that
is that New York is not America.

MRS. KRULL

It's an element in our country of which every
true American is heartily ashamed.

KRULL

Conduct that is tolerated and even applauded
here is not swallowed quite so easily out where we
come from, and if the voters of our State heard
that my daughter had involved herself with the
very type of rich, licentious club-man that they
see in the movies . . .

EMMA

They'd say that the Krull family is getting
somewhere socially at last.

Mrs. Krull

You're very smart, Emma—too smart, like most of your generation. But you know nothing about public sentiment in South Dakota.

Krull

The idea of your marrying anyone from New York is bad enough, in view of how our people feel about this place. But this one! Why, he represents everything that is despicable and contempt . . .

Emma

Excuse me, Pop—but I'm in danger of getting mad and saying things to you and mother that I'd be awfully sorry for. Can't we postpone this discussion?

Mrs. Krull

There's nothing to discuss. You've heard our views.

Krull

And even if they seem ridiculous to you, Emmy, I'm confident that you want to do what we believe to be right.

Emma

I hope so, Pop. . . . I'll go and get dressed. . . . (*She goes out, into her bedroom.*)

Krull (*to* Mrs. Krull)

You're too harsh with her. You overdo it.

Mrs. Krull

If I were her father, I'd spank her. She has the mind of a child and she needs to be treated just that way.

Krull

Well, there's one thing we've both got to remember in dealing with Emmy. It's partially our own fault if she's independent, headstrong . . .

Mrs. Krull

Our fault! Have we ever encouraged her to be anything but a dutiful, Christian daughter as she should be . . .?

Krull

No, but we've neglected her. That's the bitter penalty we've had to pay for the distinction we've gained. I with my public duties, and you with your D. A. R., and your W. C. T. U., and your Federation of Women's Clubs. . . . Why, the child has never had a real home. She's grown up here in the East, gone to Eastern schools, been exposed to all the influences that she'd never have heard of in the normal course of events back home. No wonder she's collected a lot of false standards.

Mrs. Krull

Harvey. . . . Do you suppose there has been . . . anything—that we ought to know about?

KRULL

Are you implying that our little girl could have done—could have gone to the extent of . . .?

MRS. KRULL

It isn't pleasant to harbor such suspicions. But modern youth is beyond all understanding. We never know how far they really go. This young man may have led her on to all sorts of lengths.

KRULL (*agitated*)

I admit that the same thought has crossed my mind.

MRS. KRULL

He's the sort that considers nothing as being sacred.

KRULL

I'd like to believe that my daughter is above suspicion.

MRS. KRULL

You'd like to believe it. But you know only too well that you can't. The clothes she wears, the blasphemous way she talks, the constant cigarettes, and the drinking . . .

KRULL

Oh, Lord, don't parade all the rotten evidence before me. (*He goes to the window and looks at the Chrysler Building.*) It's New York that's doing this to our country. New York—with its incalculable influence for evil. Poisoning our children with its religion of cynical sophistication. (*He suddenly realizes that he is making a strong speech.*) If I had my way, they wouldn't be given time to secede. They'd be kicked out of the Union, and let them tow their island over to Europe, where it belongs.

MRS. KRULL

Don't strain your voice. You mustn't be hoarse this evening.

KRULL

We've got to take her back home, at once, and keep her there. If we don't, there's no telling what scrapes she'll get herself into . . . and one taint of scandal on my name would drive every church-going woman in South Dakota into the arms of the Democrats. (*The telephone rings.*)

MRS. KRULL (*nervously*)

There's the 'phone.

KRULL

Probably another reporter. You take it. I won't see him.

MRS. KRULL (*at the telephone*)

Hello. . . . Who is it? (*Startled, she covers the mouthpiece with her hand.*) It's him! It's that Gresham—to see Emmy.

Krull

He can't see her.

Mrs. Krull

Hello. . . . I'm very sorry but . . .

Krull

Wait a minute. If we deny her, it'll just make her wild and she's liable to . . .

Mrs. Krull (*covering the mouthpiece again*)

If you're ever going to take a firm stand, you'd better take it now.

Krull

Tell him to come up. I'll talk to him.

Mrs. Krull

I'm not at all sure that that's the wise thing . . .

Krull

Leave it to me!

Mrs. Krull

Hello. . . . You're to come up. (*She hangs up the receiver.*) There's no need to tell Emma just yet that he's here.

Krull

Now, Edith—I have assured you that you can leave this entirely to me. (*The sight of the supper table annoys him.*) I wish they'd clear this mess out of here.

MRS. KRULL

I'll send for the waiter.

KRULL

It's that button marked room service. You push it.

MRS. KRULL (*having pushed the button*)

He has no *right* to come here like this! He's subjecting us to undesirable publicity. Suppose he had arrived when that reporter was interviewing you. For all we know, that reporter is still outside, watching. . . .

KRULL

I'm prepared to run some risks for Emmy's sake. She got herself into this, but it's up to *me* to get her out.

MRS. KRULL

You'll be soft with him, just as you are with Emmy.

KRULL

I shall talk to him exactly as though he were a delegation of Frenchmen, requesting a cancellation of the war debt!

MRS. KRULL

I only hope and pray that *she* stays in her room until you have disposed of him. (*There is a knock at the door.*)

Krull

You admit him.

(MRS. KRULL *goes to the outer door and opens it.*)

Mrs. Krull

Come in.

(JOE GRESHAM *comes in. He is a personable young man, tall, thin, sunburnt, well dressed and cheerful. He carries his hat in one hand and his stick in the other.*)

Joe

Oh, good evening, Mrs. Krull. (*He transfers his cane from right hand to left, and shakes hands with her.*) Good evening, Senator. I—I was afraid you'd both have gone on to the banquet before I got here.

Krull

Good evening.

Joe

It's a rare treat to see you here in New York, Senator. (*He shakes hands with* KRULL.)

Krull

Happily rare.

Joe

Well—I don't blame you. It's a terrible place. It didn't used to be so bad, but it's just unbelievable now. Whenever I'm here, I spend all my time trying to find an excuse to get out. (*He*

is being very affable—making a conscientious ef-
fort to divide his remarks evenly between the
SENATOR and MRS. KRULL. The latter has sat
down on the front edge of the lesser easy chair,
and is awaiting developments.)

KRULL

Will you take a seat?

JOE

Oh—thanks. (*He puts his hat and stick down*
somewhere and sits down. KRULL remains stand-
ing, at the right. JOE is beginning to be uncom-
fortably aware that all is not well.) Are you
staying in town long, Mrs. Krull?

MRS. KRULL

We're leaving on the ten o'clock train to-morrow morning.

JOE

Oh, you mustn't do that. I've been hoping to
persuade Em to bring you down to the country.
It's much better down there. You don't get the
Chrysler Building in your eye.

KRULL

We are going home.

JOE

To South Dakota?

MRS. KRULL (*with superb finality*)
Yes!

JOE

I'd love to go out there some time. The nearest I've been to it is Wyoming and I'll never forget . . .

KRULL (*ominously*)

Mr. Gresham . . .

JOE (*obviously bracing himself*)

Yes, sir?

KRULL

We have been made aware of certain—intentions, on your part, toward our daughter.

JOE

Oh! Em has told you.

KRULL

She has confirmed the rumor which was first brought to our attention through the columns of the press.

JOE

I know, Senator. It was that little bounder, Winchell. Honestly, Mrs. Krull, there's absolutely no way of knowing how he gets hold of these things.

KRULL

The source of his information is immaterial. All that concerns us is the unfortunate fact that his information happens to be correct.

JOE

That word "unfortunate" doesn't sound very promising.

MRS. KRULL

Why do you wish to marry our daughter?

KRULL

Now, Edith! I don't think we need to dwell on . . .

JOE

It's a perfectly legitimate question, sir. I understand that you want to know all about—about everything—and I hope there isn't anything that I can't tell you. (*He turns to* MRS. KRULL.) I'm in love with her. That's really the most important . . .

MRS. KRULL

You've only known her a short time.

JOE

Practically three months. I've been proposing to her steadily since almost the first day.

MRS. KRULL

And she refused you?

JOE

At least eight hundred times.

KRULL

What made her decide to change her mind?

JOE

God only knows. She must have grown sorry for me.

KRULL

Mr. Gresham. . . . I'm aware that certain old-fashioned standards of conduct are no longer generally enforced. Young people nowadays don't consider it necessary to advise their parents of their matrimonial plans until those plans have ap-proached, or even passed, fruition.

JOE

I know, Senator. It does look as if we'd tried to be secretive about it. But the fact is, I haven't been at all sure that—that Em was sure she'd marry me. And I'm afraid I'm still a little uncertain about it.

KRULL

I am in a position to relieve that uncertainty.

JOE

Has she said definitely that she really means to . . .?

KRULL

I must inform you that your engagement to Emma is at an end.

JOE

What?

MRS. KRULL

We do not wish our daughter to be married to you.

Joe

But, really . . . I don't see . . . why not?

Krull

It is not necessary or desirable for us to be explicit. We merely state our decision.

Mrs. Krull

And it is final!

Joe

Oh. You don't like me.

Krull

It is my duty, in all candor, to say that we do not.

Joe

But you don't know me. You haven't given me enough of a chance to make myself agreeable, and popular. . . .

Krull

You have the misfortune to be conspicuous, in your own set and your own district. . . .

Mrs. Krull

We've heard too many things that are not to your credit.

Krull

If your reputation has been unjustly gained, I'm sure that Mrs. Krull and I will be glad to be advised of the facts.

Joe

I don't even know what my reputation is.

Mrs. Krull

You were dismissed from Yale University.

Joe

Oh, that. . . . Well, I'm afraid that was a bit irregular.

Krull

And if I'm not entirely mistaken, there was an incident in Paris, which necessitated the intervention of our Department of State . . .

Joe

I know. If dear old Mr. Herrick hadn't stepped in and squared matters with the gendarmes, I'd have probably been condemned to Devil's Island. . . . Em knows all about these things—and they don't seem to worry her. . . .

Mrs. Krull

Emma's principles are still underdeveloped.

Joe

Oh, no, they're not, Mrs. Krull. I really don't think you know her as well as I do.

Mrs. Krull

That is a piece of impertinence that is perfectly in accord with all that I've heard of . . .

Joe

I beg your pardon. I meant no impertinence. In fact, I'm trying my damnedest to be on my very best behavior. I realize that I've made an ass of myself—on numerous occasions—but I should think you could trust Em, your own daughter, to change all that. She's determined to kick all the silly, sub-freshman nonsense out of me—and if you really understood her character, you'd be certain she could do it. . . . Honestly, Mrs. Krull—I'm not so bad at heart. Ask my own mother if I am.

Mrs. Krull

We have not the pleasure of your mother's acquaintance.

Joe

You should have. You must have. She's a pretty formidable old party, like your . . . like lots of nice elderly people. She thinks I'm awful, but not hopeless.

(Emma *comes in.*)

Emma

Ah! So it's burst. . . . Poor Joe! I'd have done anything to have spared you from this.

Joe

We've—we've just been thrashing things out.

Emma

I'll bet. . . . Is the engagement broken?

MRS. KRULL

Yes!

JOE

It is not!

KRULL

We've outlined our position to your—to Mr. Gresham.

MRS. KRULL

There is nothing more to be said on either side. (*There is a knock on the door.*)

KRULL

Who's that?
(*The* WAITER *appears.*)

WAITER

Are you finished with the . . .

KRULL

No, we're not finished! Come back later.

WAITER

Yes, sir. (*He places the check on the table and goes out.*)

EMMA

Well—if it's all over . . .

JOE

It isn't all over. We haven't even begun to . . .

MRS. KRULL

The matter has been settled.

Emma

There's one favor I'd like to ask, Pop. Give me a chance to say good-by to him, please. I mean—it's perfectly conventional for the lovers to have a good cry together before parting.

Joe

But I haven't the slightest intention of saying good-by. . . .

Emma

Shut up! Pop—will you please lead mother from the room?

Krull

Come, honey. We'll just step into the bedroom and give 'em a couple of minutes to get it over with.

Mrs. Krull (*to* Emma)

Very well. But we have no time to spare.

Krull

Make it short. (*He holds open the bedroom door as* Mrs. Krull *goes out.*)

Emma

And, Pop—would you mind knocking before you come back?

Krull

All right. (*He goes, closing the door behind him.* Joe *goes to* Emma, *takes her in his arms and kisses her.*)

Joe

I wish I'd led a better life.

Emma

I hope you're not going to tell me that you took any of that seriously?

Joe

I ought to be hardened to it. Last night I had to go through the same scene with *my* family.

Emma

Were they furious?

Joe

Yes. They too had their attention called to that piece in *The Mirror*.

Emma

What did they say?

Joe

Oh, you can imagine.

Emma

Poor things. I've had a mental picture of the expression that would come over your mother's face when she heard you were engaged to some-one named Emma Krull. (*She shudders.*)

Joe

I told them all about your father being the celebrated senator,

EMMA

That must have helped! It was like saying, "the daughter of one of our most distinguished morticians."

JOE

Well—there's nothing they can do about it.

EMMA

They can make themselves very unpleasant.

JOE

Of course they can. But there's no news in that. . . . There's something else, though, and it's a whole lot worse. . . .

EMMA

What is it? If it's my family, don't worry about them. I'll handle that end of the problem.

JOE

No, it's something terrible. . . . Em, darling— I haven't told you everything about my—my entanglements.

EMMA

You've told me enough. Anything more would be pure velvet.

JOE

There is something more, and it's just simply ghastly. . . .

EMMA

A woman?

JOE

Yes. She has claims.

EMMA

You were engaged to her?

JOE

No—but I paid her rent. I'm still paying it.

EMMA

Am I supposed to be pained—or horrified—or
what?

JOE

I haven't had anything to do with her since.
. . . But she'd always been decent with me, and I
couldn't bring myself to cut her off. I kept on
sending her checks, and best wishes. . . . Oh—
I've been the damnedest kind of damned fool!

EMMA

You don't need to be so upset, Joe. But there's
one thing I would appreciate, very much. I wish
you'd get rid of her now. . . . I hope you don't
think I'm being narrow-minded about it. . . .

JOE

That's just the trouble. I *can't* get rid of her!

EMMA

What—is she in love with you?

JOE

No! Anything but that.

EMMA

Then pay her off. You can do that, can't you?

JOE

I could if she'd be half way decent about it. But she won't. She's a tough baby. She wants one hundred thousand dollars. She says it must be paid, all of it, at once, or she'll have the whole story smeared over the tabloids.

EMMA

A hundred thousand! She *is* tough.

JOE

I can't raise that much, unless I go to father about it. There are some things he'd have to sign.

EMMA

I can imagine there might be a few complications.

JOE

Of course he's willing to do a lot to keep me out of a breach-of-promise suit—ordinarily. But not this time. The way he took on last night, he wouldn't lift a finger to make it all right for me to marry you. . . . I've got to pay her myself.

EMMA

Can't you beat her down a little?

JOE

No—she's sized up the situation beautifully. She knows all about my family and yours, too, and she's figured just how anxious we all are to avoid any suggestion of scandal.

EMMA

How did she find out?

JOE

She read that damned announcement in Winchell's column.

EMMA

We have him to thank for a lot, haven't we?

JOE

If it weren't for the fact that your father's a U. S. senator, I'd tell her to go ahead and sue, and I know she'd be glad to compromise. . . .
(*There is a knock at the door.* EMMA *goes to the door and opens it a little way.*)

KRULL (*from the bedroom*)

It's time for us to go.

EMMA

Not yet, Pop. Those things always begin late. (*She closes the door.*) Have you talked to her about it?

JOE

Have I! I was there all afternoon, arguing and threatening. . . .

EMMA

And she held out for a hundred thousand?

JOE

She did.

EMMA

Who is this wonder woman?

JOE

You may have heard of her. Her name is Phyllis Adrian.

EMMA

Phyllis Adrian. . . . Oh, if I only had a name like that!

JOE

I think she picked it out of a story in the *Cosmopolitan.*

EMMA

Is she somebody on the stage?

JOE

She works in the chorus, off and on. She's one of those impressive ones that walk down the staircase with nothing on but diamonds.

EMMA

Where do you—maintain her?

JOE

In an apartment on Central Park West.

Emma

What's she like?

Joe

Well—she's sort of . . . Oh, I don't know. What difference does it make?

Emma

Never mind, Joe. Don't try to describe her. I'm sure she's desperately attractive. You wouldn't have taken up with her if she weren't. You see—that's just conceit that makes me say that.

Joe

She *is* attractive—and I always thought she was a good sport. . . .

Emma

By that I take it you mean a good loser.

Joe

I'm in wrong enough as it is. And she's just the kind that wouldn't hesitate to get me in worse. She'll lie through her teeth about my heartless desertion—and everybody will believe every word of it. I'm in a terrible fix—and the fact that it's all my own fault doesn't make it any easier. . . . If I can't raise that money—and I can't . . .

(*There is another peremptory knock from the bedroom.*)

Emma (*at the door*)

Can't you be patient, Pop?

MRS. KRULL

We have to leave this minute.

EMMA

All right—we're almost through. (*She shuts the door.*)

JOE

Em. . . . Would you be willing to go some place, and marry me, and take the consequences?

EMMA

No, Joe—I couldn't quite do that.

JOE

Why not? Lots of people have gone through messes like this and come out alive, and even happy. . . .

EMMA

No, Joe—there's something in this that you don't understand, and that I haven't time to explain. It's the quality of public sentiment in the State of South Dakota. . . . Sometimes I think that the best thing that could happen to me, and to the United States, would be to have Pop beaten for re-election. But it would just kill him, and mother, too. She's the one who lines up the women's vote for him, and if he lost . . .

JOE

All right. I'll get her to shut up if it costs me everything I have in the . . .

EMMA

Go around there now, Joe, and see her. Plead with her. Throw yourself on her mercy. Humble yourself before her. Show her my picture . . .

JOE

She's seen your picture in *Town and Country*. That's one of the reasons for the high price. . . .
(*There is a knock on the door, and* MRS. KRULL *comes in, followed presently by the* SENATOR.)

MRS. KRULL

We're late already for that banquet. . . .

EMMA

Then you'd better hurry. I'll be up when you get back.

MRS. KRULL (*to* JOE)

I hardly think it advisable for you to remain in this room. . . .

JOE

It's perfectly all right, Mrs. Krull. It's a sitting room. The house detectives don't object if it's a suite.

KRULL (*who has been getting his black felt hat*)

Young man—I am not in the least interested in the moral code prevalent among house detectives. I must ask you to leave, before we do.

EMMA

You'd better go quietly, Joe.

MRS. KRULL

And not return during our absence.

JOE

If you wish me not to, Mrs. Krull, of course I won't. But poor Em can't stay here all alone all evening. . . .

EMMA

Never mind me, Joe. You have other duties. I'll curl up with a book until the broadcast starts. . . .

JOE (*disconsolate*)

Very well. . . . Good-by, Mrs. Krull.
(MRS. KRULL *nods and moves her lips.*)

KRULL

I'll say one thing, Gresham. I like the manly way you've taken this. (*He extends his hand.*) Good-by. . . . (*They shake hands.*)

JOE

Thank you, Senator. I was very anxious to make a good impression. (*He starts out.*)

EMMA

Keep on being manly, Joe. You may accomplish something.

JOE

Yes—I may. (*He is not happy as he goes out.*)

KRULL

Emmy—I want you to know that we feel badly about this. Your mother and I have just been regretting the fact that, in a measure, we haven't been entirely fair with you. We realize that we've never given you the kind of solid home that a girl of your age needs. . . .

EMMA

That's all right, Pop. I don't want a home.

MRS. KRULL

Are you going to start?

KRULL

Just a minute, honey. . . . There's one thing you haven't told us, Em. Do you love this young man?

EMMA

Well—I suppose . . . please, Pop—that's a pretty embarrassing question.

MRS. KRULL

It seems to me, Emma, that you're not entirely sure of your own mind.

KRULL

Your mother is right. Now, after we've finished with this Boston trip, we'll go on out to Sioux Falls and settle down among our own people and think things over for a few months, eh?

EMMA

Until after election day.

MRS. KRULL

Come on.

EMMA

Good-by, Pop. I hope the speech goes over big. (*She kisses him.*)

KRULL

You're not so bad as you like to think you are, eh, Em?

EMMA

Probably not.

MRS. KRULL

And if that young man tries to get in here again, you won't see him?

EMMA

You can count on me, Mother.

KRULL

Of course we can. (*The two of them go out.*) (EMMA *goes to the writing desk and opens the telephone book—first to the A's. She fails to find what she is looking for. Then she turns to the E's. There is a knock on the door.*)

EMMA

Who is it? . . . Oh. . . . (*She sees it is the* WAITER.) Come in. (*He comes in.* EMMA *has picked up the telephone.*) Barclay 3211.

WAITER

May I take this now, Miss?

EMMA

Yes—go ahead.

WAITER

Thank you. (*He and the* BUS-BOY *start removing the table.*)

EMMA

Hello. . . . Is this *The Evening Telegram?* I want to speak to somebody important. . . . I say, I'd like to speak to whoever it is that sends out the reporters. . . . Yes—I guess so. . . . (*To the* WAITERS.) Will you please be as quiet as . . . Hello. . . . Could you possibly tell me the name of the gentleman who was sent to the Hotel Roosevelt this evening to interview Senator Krull? . . . Senator K-R-U-L-L. . . . Yes—a little while ago. . . . What? . . . Hauser? . . . Do you suppose I could speak to him? . . . Thank you. . . .

WAITER (*hovering with the check*)

Do you wish to sign, Miss?

EMMA

Give it to me. . . . Hello, Mr. Hauser? . . . This is Senator Krull's daughter. You know, the one you helped with the soup. . . . Yes. . . . I'm sorry to bother you, but there's something

I've got to find out. Can you be trusted? . . .
Are you sure of that? . . . Good! Have you ever
heard of a lady named Phyllis Adrian? She's a
chorus girl—one of the impressive ones. . . .
I'm anxious to get in touch with her, and I
thought you might happen to know her address.
. . . Yes. . . . Oh, would you? . . . You're terribly kind. . . . Yes—I will. . . . (*She signs the
check, and speaks to the* WAITER.) My handbag
is on the dressing table in that bedroom. Will
you please bring it here?

WAITER

Yes, Miss. (*He goes out, left.*)

EMMA

Yes—I'm holding the line. Don't cut me
off. . . .

CURTAIN

ACT II

ACT II

The scene is the living room of Phyllis Adrian's *apartment on the nineteenth floor of a building on Central Park West. It is very new and, of course, self-consciously modern in its decoration. Everything in it—the furniture, lamps, bric-à-brac—would seem to have been delivered, in one load, from the Au Quatrième department at Wanamaker's.*

It is a corner apartment, facing southeast, and arranged so that there is a large bay window, in the upstage left angle of the scene, which looks out across the park toward the Plaza.

At the right, upstage, is a door leading into the dining room. Downstage, right, is a door opening onto the hall, which leads to the main entrance and also to the kitchen. At the left is a door leading to the bedroom.

At the right is a small table on which is a radio set. In the centre is a couch, and behind it a refectory table. Another small table at the left bears the one-piece telephone.

There are various ornamental chairs about, and art work on the walls to match. There is a tall mirror on the wall at the left.

71

LUCILLE, *the colored servant, is sitting on the couch, reading* The Daily Mirror. *She is neat and respectable-looking, and wears pince-nez eyeglasses. The radio is going; it is some pianist, rendering "By the Waters of the Minnetonka." The door at the left is open.*

The time is somewhat later in the same evening as Act I.

PHYLLIS ADRIAN'S *voice is heard from the left.*

PHYLLIS
Hey, Lucille. . . .

LUCILLE
Yes, Miss Phil.

PHYLLIS
Haven't we had about enough of that?

LUCILLE
Yes, Miss Phil. (*She goes and shuts off the radio, and returns to her perusal of* The Mirror.)

PHYLLIS
What's that you're reading?

LUCILLE
It's *The Mirror.*

PHYLLIS
Don't you ever read anything else?

LUCILLE (*placidly*)

No, Miss Phil.

(PHYLLIS *comes in from the bedroom. She is slim, graceful, studiously poised and only partially dressed. She is trying to fasten the clasp of her choker pearl necklace.*)

PHYLLIS

What's the news?

LUCILLE

It says here that Miss Dorothy's expectin' a blessed event.

PHYLLIS

Blessed! That wasn't the word *she* used when she told me about it.

LUCILLE

I s'pose not. Well—she'll know better next time.

PHYLLIS

Fasten this, will you. (*She is facing the mirror, at the left.*)

LUCILLE

Yes, Miss Phil. (*She goes to fasten the clasp.*) You goin' out?

PHYLLIS

There's a party upstairs. I may go up for a while. (*She regards herself in the mirror.*) God, I look wonderful!

LUCILLE

Yes, Miss Phil. (*She completes the fastening.*)

PHYLLIS

Thanks. (*She goes back into the bedroom. The doorbell is heard from the right.* LUCILLE *folds The Mirror and places it on the refectory table. Then she goes out at the right to open the door.* HARRY GLASSMAN *comes in. He is an urbane gorilla, attired in a stylish double-breasted dinner jacket with a soft silk shirt. His sleek black hair is graying. He is smoking a good cigar.*)

GLASSMAN (*as he is coming in*)

Hello, Lucille.

LUCILLE

Good evenin', Mr. Glassman.

GLASSMAN

Miss Adrian in?

PHYLLIS (*from the bedroom*)

Hello, Harry.

GLASSMAN

Hi, Phil.

PHYLLIS

I'm getting dressed for your party. . . . Lucille! (LUCILLE *crosses and goes into the bedroom.*) Sit down, Harry. How's things?

GLASSMAN

All right, I guess.

PHYLLIS

That sounds like not so good.

GLASSMAN

I lost a boat off Montauk this morning. Six
thousand cases. I guess the Coast Guard is cock-
eyed drunk to-night. (*He sits down and picks up
The Evening Graphic, turning to the dramatic
section.*) That Theatre Guild show got wonderful notices.

PHYLLIS

Did you go to the opening?

GLASSMAN

I did. And it was a honey. If they don't do
any better pretty soon I'm going to cancel my
subscription.

PHYLLIS

I read what that Atkinson said about it in *The
Times*.

GLASSMAN

Did he like the show?

PHYLLIS

I couldn't make out. . . . How's Clarisse?

GLASSMAN

Clarisse is in bad shape.

PHYLLIS

Oh, I'm sorry to hear that. . . . Hey! Look
out for that pin!

LUCILLE

Now you ain't hurt yet, Miss Phil.

PHYLLIS

What seems to be the chief trouble with her?

GLASSMAN

She's been hitting it again.

PHYLLIS

No!

GLASSMAN

I thought I had her watched all right—but somehow or other she got in touch with that dirty Greek. She's on the rampage up there.

(PHYLLIS *has wandered in, still dressing with* LUCILLE'S *help.*)

PHYLLIS

She'll quiet down.

GLASSMAN

The worst of it is—I've got to go on a trip to Prince Edward Island to-morrow. We're opening up a new base there. And she wants to go along. . . . Well, now—hell—you know I can't have her on my hands, on a boat, with a lot of tricky business to be done. But can I tell *her* that?

PHYLLIS

You ought to be thankful to have somebody as crazy about you as that.

GLASSMAN

I sometimes wish to God she'd get sick of me. . . .

PHYLLIS

No, you don't. You'll always be a sap about her. . . . Well—it just goes to show that even a gorilla has human weaknesses. (*She goes back into her room.* GLASSMAN *gets up and walks around the room.*)

GLASSMAN

Oh, well—I should be bothering you with my troubles, when you've got plenty of your own.

PHYLLIS

I'm not worrying.
(*This and subsequent speeches are from off-stage.*)

GLASSMAN

Has Joe given you your notice yet?

PHYLLIS

Yes—he was up this afternoon. Said I could go on living here forever, if I wanted to.

GLASSMAN

Joe's a nice boy. I wish my kid would grow up to be like him—well educated, and snappy. . . .

PHYLLIS

Your kid?

GLASSMAN

You didn't know I had one, did you? Well—
I have. He lives out on the Coast, with his mother.
He plays polo, too. He's going to enter the University of Southern California next fall. I wanted
him to come East and go to Harvard or Yale, or
one of those high-class schools. But I guess my
ex-wife wanted to keep him as far as possible
away from me.

PHYLLIS

Do you blame her?

GLASSMAN

No—I don't. . . . She's even changed her
name—to Glaezer—so when the news breaks that
I've been bumped off, the boy won't even know
it's his own old man. . . .

(PHYLLIS *appears in the doorway again.*)

PHYLLIS

Nobody's going to bump you off, Harry. . . .

GLASSMAN

No? They got Rothstein, didn't they?

PHYLLIS

Well—if they do get you, I hope it'll be your
own friends that do it, and not the law. (*She
goes back into the bedroom.*)

GLASSMAN

Say—the law is the best pal I've got. . . .
Did you call up that smart lawyer I told you
about?

PHYLLIS

No.

GLASSMAN

You better do it.

PHYLLIS

I'm not splitting with lawyers—not yet.

GLASSMAN

Well—you'll be a sucker to try to swing a
thing like this by yourself. You're liable to over-
play your hand. If you take my advice, you'll
turn it over to Nick Pinanski *now*, and do everything he tells you. He's settled plenty of cases
exactly like this before. Why, the muggs shiver
at the sound of his name.

(*The front door is heard to open and close.*
JOE *comes in.*)

JOE

Oh—hello, Harry.

GLASSMAN

Why, hello, Joe!

JOE

Where's Phil?

PHYLLIS

Hello, sweets. I'll be right out.

(JOE *has wandered over to the left, glanced*

*into the bedroom, and then turned away. He is
obviously distracted.*)

GLASSMAN (*very genial*)

Well—what do you think of Federal Power to-
day?

JOE

I haven't seen a paper. What did it do?

GLASSMAN

A new low! (*He laughs.*)

JOE

Were you on it?

GLASSMAN

I certainly was.

JOE

Too bad.

GLASSMAN

Well—I took the loss and pulled out. . . . By
the way, Joe—I want to offer my congratula-
tions. . . .

JOE

What for?

GLASSMAN

I've heard some pretty marvellous news about
you. They tell me you're contemplating matrimony.

JOE

Oh—yes. . . .

GLASSMAN

I don't happen to know the young lady in question, but I've seen her pictures plenty of times in the papers, and she looks good. . . . I mean, I certainly congratulate you.

JOE

Thanks very much.

GLASSMAN

It's a great little state, matrimony. I haven't been there in years, but I can tell you it's a lot better than it's made out to be. There are plenty of things that's worse. (*He accompanies this sage observation with a glance upward.* PHYLLIS *comes in, fully dressed.*)

PHYLLIS

Well, sweets—it's a surprise seeing you here.

JOE

Yes—it is.

GLASSMAN

I suppose you want me to bow out at this point.

PHYLLIS

No, Harry. You stick around.

GLASSMAN

I tell you what. Why don't the two of you come on upstairs to my place. The rest of the gang will be along any minute and we can . . .

PHYLLIS

Yes. I know what you want. You want to have us as escort when you face Clarisse.

GLASSMAN

You're a fine neighbor!

JOE

If you don't mind, Harry—I haven't got much time, and there's something I've got to talk to Phil about. So, if you don't mind. . . .

GLASSMAN

Not at all, Joe. Far be it from me to be the third party.

PHYLLIS (*to* JOE)

Is it so personal as all that?

JOE

Yes.

GLASSMAN (*at the door*)

But will you please come up soon?

PHYLLIS

Sure.

GLASSMAN

'By, Joe. (*He goes out.*)

(JOE *has sat down on the couch.* PHYLLIS *stands behind him and strokes his hair.*)

PHYLLIS

Well—what's on the little mind now?

JOE

Cut it out. (*He brushes her hand away.*)

PHYLLIS

Oh——you rough thing!

JOE

You know damned well what's on my mind.

PHYLLIS

Yes——and I've told you just how to get it off,
haven't I, sweets?

JOE

And don't call me sweets! I never did like that
word. Now, it's just simply nauseating.

PHYLLIS

You've got to forgive me, Joe, if I can't help
being a little sentimental. You see, it isn't so
easy for me to realize that all our happy times
are over. I've been thinking about them . . .
those rides we used to take down to Long Beach
on hot nights, and all those cozy little suppers at
Reuben's and——and, well, I'm afraid I cried a little. . . .

(JOE *gives her a look, but makes no comment
on that statement.*)

JOE

I came here to tell you that there's absolutely
nothing doing on that deal of yours.

PHYLLIS

No?

JOE

I haven't got a hundred thousand dollars.

PHYLLIS

I've heard different.

JOE

You've heard wrong.

PHYLLIS

What's become of all that dough? Has the Chase National Bank failed?

JOE

You couldn't begin to understand all the difficulties there are. . . . Have you ever met my father?

PHYLLIS

No, I haven't. But any time you want to bring him up, I'll be only too pleased to. . . .

JOE

Oh, for God's sake, Phil. . . . Haven't you got a spark of common kindness in that ice-box of a heart of yours? You ought to realize that I'll give you just as much as I possibly can.

PHYLLIS

If I only had myself to think of, it would be different. We'd part with a handshake and not another word. But there are others. . . .

Joe

Yes—I know. There's your old mother, and your thousands of little brothers and sisters, and their ailments. I've already staked the whole outfit to at least six operations apiece, and I don't know how many trips to California. What's the matter with them now?

Phyllis

The doctors say they *have* to be moved to the south of France.

Joe

All of them?

Phyllis

All except little Fred—and if he doesn't get into the Alps at once, it may be too late. . . .

Joe

Now listen, Phil. Suppose I tell you on my word of honor that I'll raise every last cent I can —every last cent. It might be as much as forty or fifty thousand. Whatever it is, I swear it's all yours. . . .

Phyllis

You're very white, Joe. I've known that all along. You're as white a man as God ever created, and I only wish there were a few more like you. But there aren't, Joe. There aren't enough decent, on-the-level gentlemen to go 'round. And that's why I'm holding out for one hundred grand.

(JOE *goes to the window and contemplates the electric signs on 59th Street.*) What are you looking at, Joe?

JOE

At the General Motors sign. . . . "The Most Significant Chevrolet in Chevrolet History." . . . As if anybody cared! (*This seems to inspire him to an outburst of courageous vehemence. He turns on her.*) All right, hold out for your hundred thousand. Hold out forever, and see what it gets you. Not a damned nickel out of me—and a lot of lawyers' fees out of your own fat bank account. Because you know you haven't got any case if it ever comes to court. . . .

PHYLLIS

I don't need a case. All I need is a good lawyer—and I'm going to get one.

JOE

Who?

PHYLLIS

You'll find out. If you want to be a little soldier about it, and take your licking, why take it, and lose this South Dakota débutante you're so . . .

JOE

You don't know what you're talking about.

PHYLLIS

I don't, eh! I guess that ham senator from the West will stand by you when your name is being dragged through the dirt. I guess your own father will stand by you. Yes!

JOE

What kind of story are you going to cook up? I suppose it'll be that I promised you marriage, and then stole your poor little virtue.

PHYLLIS

It'd be pretty hard to prove that you didn't.

JOE

Impossible—but I hope you won't stop at anything as obvious and simple as that. You know, to get any attention in this town nowadays you've got to make me out some kind of a fiend. You ought to be able to do that, with your nasty mind.

PHYLLIS

You think I'm pretty cruel, don't you?

JOE

That's my impression.

PHYLLIS

Well, you aren't far wrong. . . . I'll be honest with you, Joe—and tell you that I wouldn't even treat a dog the way I'm going to treat you.

And do you want to know why? It's because I've never yet seen a dog that had any money. . . . And I'm not falling for that hard-times gag, either. One hundred thousand dollars is a drop in the bucket with you, and you know it, and so do I. And if I don't get it before Wednesday noon, my affairs go into the hands of Mr. Nicholas Pinanski, of Callahan, Pinanski & Hughes.

(JOE *regards her with loathing for a while, then turns and strides to the door.*)

JOE

Good-by, you bitch! (*He goes out.* PHYLLIS *follows him to the hall entrance.*)

PHYLLIS

Good night, sweets. (*The slam of the front door is heard. . . . After a moment,* PHYLLIS *calls,* "*Lucille.*" LUCILLE *is heard to answer,* "*Yes, Miss Phil.*") What was the station where they were going to broadcast that speech?

(LUCILLE *has come in. She goes to consult The Mirror.*)

LUCILLE

It was JZ, I think. (*While* LUCILLE *is searching the radio column,* PHYLLIS *goes to the radio, at the right.*) Yes—WJZ, "Banquet of Society of Sons of the Northwest, Hotel Astor, 9 P.M."

(PHYLLIS *has been tuning in on WJZ, passing one or two stations on the way. The resonant voice of* KRULL *booms forth from the loud speaker. It is much too loud at first, but is softened by* PHYLLIS's *manipulation of the volume control.*)

KRULL

For a hundred and fifty-four years, since the first, faint rays of golden light heralded the dawn of liberty, Europe has looked upon these United States with frank and confident scorn. Among the sovereign nations of the Old World, our country has been regarded as a red-headed step-child. (*Laughter.*)

PHYLLIS

I guess that's him.

LUCILLE

It certainly is. I heard him lots of times on the radio when he was talkin' against Al Smith.

KRULL

But now—to-day! What now is the attitude of the Old World toward us of the New? It is one, my friends, of cringing, obsequious respect. (*Applause.*)

PHYLLIS

How would you like to have that for a father-in-law?

(*The door-bell rings.* LUCILLE *goes to answer it.*)

KRULL

Within the past decade, this former step-child among nations has achieved recognition—universal recognition!—as the Big Brother of all humanity! (*Prolonged applause and cheers.*)

LUCILLE

It's a lady that wants to see you.

PHYLLIS

Who?

LUCILLE

She don't say who she is.
(EMMA *comes in.*)

EMMA

I'm terribly sorry to have to crash in like this. . . .

PHYLLIS

What do you want?

EMMA

Are you Miss Adrian?

PHYLLIS

I am—and who are you?
(*The applause has died down, and* KRULL'S *voice is again heard.*)

KRULL

We find ourselves on top of the world!
(*Startled,* EMMA *has wheeled around and seen the radio.*)

EMMA

It's Pop!

PHYLLIS

What?

KRULL

But, my friends, the position of leadership is not always an enviable one. . . .

(PHYLLIS *shuts off the radio.*)

EMMA

I beg your pardon. That voice made me jump. It's my father.

PHYLLIS (*peering at* EMMA)

Well, well! Of all people! How do you do, Miss Krull?

EMMA

How do you do, Miss Adrian?

PHYLLIS

He sent you here, didn't he?

EMMA

Who?

PHYLLIS

Joe—the big coward. . . .

EMMA

He doesn't know I'm here.

PHYLLIS

Oh, no. He just went down in the elevator this minute, and you were waiting for him outside in the taxi, weren't you? And he said, "For God's sake you go up and try to reason with her. . . ."

EMMA

I was waiting outside, but he didn't know it. I was across the street, on one of those park benches, watching for him to come out. And when he did, and I saw him drive away, I came in.

PHYLLIS

All right. We'll let it go at that. . . . Sit down, Miss Krull.

EMMA

Thanks. (*She sits.*)

PHYLLIS

Will you have a drink?

EMMA

I'd love to.

PHYLLIS

Lucille! (LUCILLE's *voice replies. Presently she appears.*) What would you like? We have Scotch, rye, champagne, liqueurs, beers. . . .

EMMA

I'm very fond of champagne.

PHYLLIS

We have tastes in common. Champagne, Lucille.

LUCILLE

Yes, Miss Phil. (*She goes to get it.* PHYLLIS *sits down.*)

PHYLLIS

So Joe told you the bad news about me, did he?

EMMA

Yes—he tells me everything—I hope.

PHYLLIS

He was even thoughtful enough to give you my address.

EMMA

Oh, no. I found that out through a friend of mine who works on a newspaper.

PHYLLIS

Well—that's possible.

EMMA

It wasn't very polite of me to come up without any warning—but—I was afraid that if I did call you beforehand you wouldn't let me in.

PHYLLIS

I don't know how I could have stopped you. After all, it's Joe who pays the rent here, and I guess you have as much right to use it as I have.

EMMA (*looking around*)

It's quite an attractive place.

PHYLLIS

It's novel.

EMMA

Did you do it yourself?

PHYLLIS

No. It was an interior decorator, Sheila Lavery. . . .

EMMA

Oh, yes.

PHYLLIS

She's queer, but she's clever. Joe got her up here one day to look the place over, and a couple of days later it was all set for me to move in.

EMMA

You must have been thrilled. . . .

PHYLLIS

What?

EMMA

I mean—it must have been just like a bride, coming in to her new home.

PHYLLIS

Well—I didn't think of that at the time.

EMMA

How many rooms have you? I hope you don't mind me being so inquisitive—but—you can imagine that I'd be interested. . . .

PHYLLIS

I don't mind at all. . . . In there's the dining room, and beyond it, the kitchen. And on this side's the bedroom. (*Indicating the left.*)

EMMA (*looking toward the bedroom*)

I see. . . . Just one bedroom?

PHYLLIS

Just one.

EMMA

You must be very comfortable.

PHYLLIS

That's my ambition.

(LUCILLE *comes in with a tray, on which are an open bottle of champagne and two glasses. She hands the drinks to* PHYLLIS *and* EMMA *and goes out.*)

EMMA

I agree with you. I've always wanted to live somewhere where there's champagne always on ice.

PHYLLIS

You'll get your wish. Joe's very lavish—in some ways.

EMMA

Well, thanks very much. (*She takes a good gulp of the champagne.*)

PHYLLIS

Don't mention it. (*She takes a more discreet sip.*) Does your father know where you are?

EMMA

Oh, no. I've got to get back to the hotel before he does. . . . I'll go now if I'm interfering with your plans at all. . . .

PHYLLIS

I'm in no hurry. You can take all the time you want getting around to the main subject.

EMMA

What main subject?

PHYLLIS

Money.

EMMA

Oh! You still think that Joe sent me here to —to reason with you?

PHYLLIS

I'm making no accusations. I'm just waiting for you to begin. . . .

EMMA

I don't even want to *mention* that subject. Joe's business affairs are no concern of mine.

Phyllis

Well—you oughtn't to worry about a little matter of a hundred grand out of Joe's roll. He'll have plenty left.

Emma

Of course he will. More than I'll ever need. . . . This is marvellous champagne.

Phyllis

It ought to be. It comes from headquarters. I've got a neighbor upstairs who's one of the biggest shots in the business. (*She is pouring some more champagne.*)

Emma

You mean a boot-legger?

Phyllis

Oh, no. He's the one the boot-leggers get it from.

Emma

I'd love to meet him.

Phyllis

That could be arranged.

Emma

I envy you, Miss Adrian. Knowing everybody, going everywhere. . . .

PHYLLIS

Now, you needn't be formal. Everybody calls
me Phil.

EMMA

Thanks. . . . There's really no reason why we
shouldn't get to be friends. We're just two girls,
in practically the same boat.

PHYLLIS

The same yacht.

EMMA

Yes—that's it. But—I'm a stranger on board.
. . . You see, Phil—I come from the Great Northwest—the wheat country. Out there, when a
young man kisses a young girl for the first time,
that's the same as . . .

PHYLLIS

I know.

EMMA

My parents never told me about the facts of
life, and you can't blame them for neglect. In
South Dakota, there aren't any facts worth re-
peating.

PHYLLIS

Well, my dear, you've come to the right place
to get an education. In this town, you learn fast.

EMMA

That's what I want to do. I want to be just
like you, and live in a place like this, on the nine-

teenth floor, with a view of Central Park, and a
big boot-legger for a neighbor.

PHYLLIS

When you get married to Joe, you won't live
in this neighborhood. You'll be on the *other* side
. . . East. . . . (*With a gesture eastward.*)

EMMA

Is it so very different on that side?

PHYLLIS

It used to be, but it's changing. The Christian
colony over there is getting smaller and smaller.

EMMA

Joe and I will have to come over here often to
see you.

PHYLLIS

Oh, I'm planning to move to Park Avenue myself, if all goes well.

EMMA

Let's hope it will.

PHYLLIS

Let's be pretty damned sure of it. . . . (*She
refills the glasses.*) Joe certainly thinks he's wild
about you.

EMMA

Do you think he is?

PHYLLIS

I know it. I can tell it by the way he acts.

EMMA

How does he act?

PHYLLIS

He takes things so seriously. He's moody. And that isn't like him. He's usually one of those what-of-it boys. But I'd like to give you one piece of advice, Emma.

EMMA

I'm crazy to hear it.

PHYLLIS

Don't let yourself fall in love with him.

EMMA

Did you?

PHYLLIS

I might have.

EMMA

Would it have been so awful if you had?

PHYLLIS

It would have been ruinous. If I'd got myself in love with him, do you think I'd have been able to stand up to him the way I'm doing now, and make him pay me off before he marries you?

EMMA

You'd have just as much of a right to get what you deserve.

PHYLLIS

More of a right. But I'd be sentimental about it. I'd say, "Go ahead, Joe—have your happiness—marry the girl you love—and don't think any more about me." And then the minute he went out the door, I'd jump out the window—another broken doll. . . . Have some more champagne. . . .

EMMA

Thanks.

PHYLLIS

You may find yourself in the same position one of these days. Not that I want to seem pessimistic, but . . .

EMMA

Oh, I know what men are.

PHYLLIS

I thought you said you didn't.

EMMA

I don't, by experience. But anyone who has ever read a book is bound to have a few suspicions on the subject.

PHYLLIS

When he does cool off, he'll come around and ask you to be a good sport about it.

EMMA

Naturally.

PHYLLIS

Don't let him get away with it. You've got to
hold out for your accident insurance, like I've
done. But you'll never be able to do it if you've
made the mistake of falling for him.

(*The door-bell rings.*)

EMMA

Who's that? It isn't Joe, is it?

PHYLLIS

Oh, no. He has a key. . . . Who is it, Lucille?
(JEAN's *strident voice is heard as the front door
opens.*)

JEAN

Hello, Lucille. . . . Are we welcome? (JEAN
*comes in. She is very girlish, but not very young;
her hair is too red. She is followed by* BABE
SAVITO, *a short, stalwart, well-groomed pug.*)

PHYLLIS

Hello, Jean. Hello, Babe.

JEAN

Hello, darling.

BABE

Hello, Phil.

JEAN

We've been up at Harry's, and, my dear, *words* can't express it.

PHYLLIS

This is a friend of mine. (*Indicating* EMMA.) Miss—Miss Jessup. (EMMA *darts a glance of gratitude at* PHYLLIS *for this display of discretion.*) Miss Doran.

JEAN

How do you do, Miss Jessup? *So* glad to know you. . . .

PHYLLIS

And Mr. Babe Savito, champion of the world. I can never remember what weight.

BABE

All weights!

JEAN

Well, my dear, the party upstairs is *sim*ply beyond words. Everybody's leaving. You can't conceive of the way Clarisse is behaving. She's got herself so full of cocaine she's *pos*itively disgusting.

BABE

If I was Harry, believe me I'd take a sock at that dame.

JEAN

It's the most revolting spectacle!

PHYLLIS

Will you sit down and have a drink?

JEAN (*looking at the tray*)

What is this, champagne? No—I've been sticking to rye.

PHYLLIS

There's some in the dining room. Lucille!
(*The door-bell rings.*)

JEAN

Never mind. We'll get it for ourselves, won't we, Babe darling?

BABE

Sure.

(JEAN *goes into the dining room, chattering gaily, followed by* BABE.)

EMMA

Who are they?

PHYLLIS

She's some kind of fancy buyer—with Macy's, I think. Spends half her time in Paris. And Babe Savito—I guess you've heard of him.

EMMA

They seem awfully nice.

PHYLLIS

Well, they're not. They're a couple of punks.
. . . Oh, hello, Judge.

(JUDGE GOHAGAN *comes in—a suave, sleek, hard-boiled, Tammany good fellow; he is in the prime of life, and enjoying it. With him is* MILT

FLIESLER, *an indistinct youth, and* SHEILA LAV-
ERY, *the queer interior decorator.* SHEILA *is very
smartly dressed, her skin is chalk white, her lips
gaudy red, and she has an ominous expression.*)

JUDGE

Hello, sweetheart. We got thrown out, upstairs. (*He kisses* PHYLLIS.)

SHEILA (*in a bored baritone*)

Hello, Phil.

JUDGE (*eyeing* EMMA)

And who's this little ornament?

PHYLLIS

This is . . . I'm terribly sorry, but I've forgotten your name.

EMMA

I think it was Jessup.

PHYLLIS

Oh, of course! Miss Jessup—Judge Gohagan,
Miss Sheila Lavery and—who's that? Oh—hello,
Milt. . . .

(*There are general greetings and bowings, not
joined in by* SHEILA.)

SHEILA

Where's Jean?

PHYLLIS

Gone into the dining room, to get some rye.

SHEILA

With that greasy prize-fighter?

PHYLLIS

Yes.

(SHEILA *strides into the dining room.*)

JUDGE

Can you beat it? She's burning!

MILT

Oh—Harry said to tell you he's sending his butler down with all the supper because he can't use it. . . .

JUDGE

He's turning the whole party over to you, including the bad will. (*To* EMMA.) Have I met you before, blondie? (*He is making a pass.*)

EMMA

No—I don't think so. (*She tries not to shrink.*)

PHYLLIS

She's just in from the Northwest. She don't know anybody here. . . .

JUDGE

Well—we got to do something about *that*, eh, baby?

Phyllis

Why don't you go on in with the others and have a drink, or something. . . .

(Lucille *comes in.*)

Milt

I'd be glad to. (*He goes into the dining room.*)

Lucille

Mr. Glassman's butler and the maid and the chef has come down with a lot a sandwiches and salad and things like that. Do you want 'em put in the dining room?

Phyllis

Yes. . . .

Judge

By all means, Lucille—because what with first one thing and then the other, I'm hungry.

Lucille (*wearily*)

All right. (*She goes out. There is plenty of talk heard from the dining room.*)

Judge

Say—there's some battle royal going on upstairs.

Phyllis

Hopped up again, is she?

Judge

To the eye-lashes.

PHYLLIS

Poor kid. I suppose I'd better go up and see if there's anything I can do. . . .

JUDGE

I wouldn't. You're liable to get hurt. She's tearing hair, throwing things, smashing up expensive early American antiques. . . . It's going to cost Harry a lot of dough. . . .

PHYLLIS

Is he with her?

JUDGE

Yeh—and he's taking it on the chin, believe me! I've been telling him for a long time he ought to get rid of that snow-bird. I mean to say, a man like Harry Glassman oughtn't to have to put up with that stuff.

PHYLLIS

Maybe he's fond of her.

JUDGE

Maybe. . . . Well—what do you say we go eat? You come along with me, cuteness, and we'll split a lettuce and tomato on rye. . . . (*He has put his arm around* EMMA *and is leading her to the dining room.*)

PHYLLIS

Hey! You go ahead, Judge. We'll follow.

JUDGE

Something private?

PHYLLIS

Yes!

JUDGE (*knowingly*)

I get you. . . . But don't forget, baby—when you come into the bar, just ask for the judge. (*He goes to the dining-room door, from which issue raucous sounds of strife.*) What's this, what's this? More fighting. Now, please, *ladies*. . . . (*He has gone out.* PHYLLIS *goes after him and closes the door.*)

PHYLLIS

Look here, girlie. I think you'd better be going on home.

EMMA

Am I in the way?

PHYLLIS

It isn't that, but . . . I don't like the looks of this little gang.

EMMA

It can't be so bad as long as there's a judge present.

PHYLLIS

The judge isn't on legal duty to-night. He's on the make—and I don't think your father would want you to learn too much all at once.

EMMA

You needn't be nervous about me, Phil. This is just the kind of party I love! Wait a minute. (*She goes to the radio and turns it on.*)

KRULL

. . . had it not been for the policy of weak-kneed vacillation in the White House, this nation would have marched on to . . .

EMMA (*switching it off*)

It's all right. Pop's still talking. I don't have to go yet. . . .

(GLASSMAN *has come in.*)

GLASSMAN

The front door was wide open, so I just walked in.

PHYLLIS

Oh, that's all right. Leave it wide open so that everybody can come in. (*He has slumped down on the couch.*) By the looks of the crowd we're getting here to-night this apartment's been put up in Joe Leblang's.

GLASSMAN

I'm sorry, Phil. But there was just no use. . . .

PHYLLIS

Never mind. . . . How's Clarisse now?

GLASSMAN

She's quieter.

PHYLLIS

That's good. Oh! Excuse me—I want you to meet my friend, Miss Jessup. This is Mr. Harry Glassman, one of our most outstanding racketeers.

GLASSMAN (*without looking up*)

Glad to meet you. . . . Where's the rest of the gang?

PHYLLIS

They're in there, some of them. The others must have gone home. . . . Would it do any good if I went upstairs and talked to Clarisse?

GLASSMAN

You can if you want to. But you might just get her started again. . . . You haven't got such a thing as any bromo seltzer, have you?

PHYLLIS

Certainly. There's some in the bathroom.

GLASSMAN (*standing up*)

I need it.

PHYLLIS

Take a couple of heaping teaspoonfuls.

GLASSMAN (*at the door*)

I'll tell you one thing, Phil: I've stood it just as long as I can stand anything. . . .

PHYLLIS

I know that, Harry. Now go on and . . .

GLASSMAN

If I thought it was my own fault that she's got
herself into this state, why, I swear to God I'd go
through with it and . . . I've put her through
two cures already and she's come out of them
worse than before. One of these days she's going
to get a hold of a gun and kill me. . . . I've got
to send her away. . . .

PHYLLIS

Is she going to like that?

GLASSMAN

No—she isn't. But it's got to be done. There's
a place out in Indiana—everybody says it's fine,
and healthy. They know how to take care of—of
people that get like that. Maybe she'll be absolutely O. K. in a couple of months. . . . Oh, jeez,
Phil—I know everybody's going to say I'm just
a rat . . . but what am I going to *do?*

PHYLLIS

Never mind, Harry. You'll only make your
headache worse. Go and take that bromo seltzer.
And lie down for a while, if you want to.

GLASSMAN

All right. (*He goes out at the left.*)

PHYLLIS

There, Emma—get a load of that little lesson.
There's a fine demonstration of what love is.

EMMA

Is that love?

PHYLLIS

Yes. That's love. That poor little floosie upstairs—the one they call Clarisse—she's just absolutely nuts about him. She eats and drinks and
breathes Harry Glassman. Can you believe it?

EMMA

He must have treated her terribly.

PHYLLIS

He has not. He's been wonderful to her. He
picked her up when she was a bum cooch dancer,
and he's given her everything. . . . But just because his business takes him out of the city a lot
. . . well, you can see what's happened. She's
taken up cocaine so that she can live through the
nights when he's away.

EMMA

How long have they been married?

PHYLLIS

They never bothered to get married. But
they've been living together for seven years. Seven
years! That's a long time in New York.

EMMA

And is he going to leave her now?

PHYLLIS

I guess so. He'll take care of her all right. He can afford it. But what good will that do her, when she can't have him?

EMMA

Is it anything like that with you and Joe?

PHYLLIS

No—nothing at all. But I'm going to make it sound like that by the time it comes out in the papers.

EMMA

It'll be a sensational story, won't it?

PHYLLIS

It'll be a beaut. But do you or don't you admit that he's got it coming to him?

(EMMA *has glanced at her watch.*)

EMMA

Look here, Phil. I haven't much more time, so I'm afraid I'll have to get to the main subject now. Do you mind?

PHYLLIS

Certainly not!

EMMA (*advancing*)

I'm glad to have had a chance to know you, Phil. It strengthens my faith in Joe's taste.

PHYLLIS

Go on, dear. I know what's coming.

EMMA

You're honest. You're not at all like what I expected. And I want to be the same with you. I'm going to marry Joe—and all the scandals you can cut loose won't stop me.

PHYLLIS

You mean you'd stick to him even if I made him the gag of the town?

EMMA

That's what I mean. You're wasting your time threatening him. The only one you can really hurt is my father—and—and certainly you haven't got anything to gain from that. You don't care who wins the next election in South Dakota. Now, listen, Phil, you've got brains—and what's more, you've got sense. You want to get what you can, and don't think I begrudge it to you; but I don't want to see you come out of this with nothing but the knowledge that you've injured a kind man who doesn't ask for anything in this world but to belong to the U. S. Senate. So I advise you to be smart and settle with Joe for whatever he can raise—because that's all you can possibly get.

(PHYLLIS *regards* EMMA *with unconcealed admiration.*)

PHYLLIS

You're a funny kid, Emma. I wonder how Joe ever happened to pick you out.

(*The* JUDGE *comes in bearing a huge platter full of sandwiches.*)

JUDGE

Say! Ain't you kids ever going to eat? (*As he leans over to hand them the platter, he says, in a low tone.*) Confidentially, we got a new uproar on our hand. . . .

(JEAN *and* SHEILA *come in, carrying highball glasses.*)

SHEILA

. . . I'll slap his filthy face. . . .

JEAN

Now, darling, will you *please* try to believe me when I . . .

BABE (*coming in*)

Well—if there's going to be any socking going on around here . . .

JUDGE

Attaboy, Babe!

SHEILA (*to* BABE)

Would you be interested in knowing exactly
what you can do, you God-damned . . .

PHYLLIS

Now, wait a minute. You ladies and gentlemen
can either behave yourselves respectably, or get
the hell out of my place.

SHEILA

Your place, you cheap kept woman. . . .

JEAN

Please, Phil, don't listen to her. She doesn't
mean any offence.

PHYLLIS

No? Maybe she only wants to get a few of her
front teeth knocked out.

JUDGE (*to* EMMA)

Just like so many nuns.

BABE (*to* PHYLLIS)

It ain't any of my doing—and I want to apologize to you, Phil. . . .

SHEILA

How charming of you.

BABE

But I just want to tell *you*, that if there's going
to be any socking around here, why . . .

SHEILA

Can't you get two words out of that Wop mouth of yours without one of them being "sock"?

JEAN

Oh, darling—*lay* off!

MILT (*coming in excitedly*)

Say, everybody! Look out the window. You can see the big Zeppelin. (*He has rushed to the window.*)

PHYLLIS

We've seen it. . . . Now are you going to cut it out, or go home—which? (*This is addressed to* SHEILA, *who doesn't deign to reply.*)

BABE

It's all the same with me. (*He wolfs a sandwich.* SHEILA *sits down on the couch and lights a cigarette.*)

JEAN

Darling—you *mustn't* be like this.

JUDGE (*singing*)

"Happy Days are here again—cha, *cha*, cha, cha . . ." (*He jazzes off into the dining room.*)

MILT (*still at the window*)

Jeez—how'd you like to cross the ocean in one of them? Some thrill, eh?

SHEILA (*to* EMMA)

What are *you* staring at?

EMMA

I beg your pardon—I . . .

PHYLLIS (*to* SHEILA)

Get out of here!

BABE

All I ask is just one sock.

PHYLLIS

You heard me.

SHEILA

I'll be glad to let you know when I'm ready to leave.

BABE

Just one—that's all I ask.

JEAN

Oh—this is *terrible!*

PHYLLIS

Are you going to walk, or do you have to be thrown?

SHEILA

If I'm not mistaken, you've been kicked out of here yourself.

(*All of this has been jumbled together in the general heat.*)

JEAN (*jumping up, with appalling gaiety*)

I tell you what. Let's have a little cheerful music. (*She starts singing jazzily herself as she turns on the radio.*)

BABE

I'd hate to sock a woman, but you're different.

SHEILA (*with a merry laugh*)

Of course—the whole thing is really very amusing!

KRULL (*from the radio*)

Europe is pouring her poison into the life blood of America—and that infection, my friends, is entering through this open wound—New York! (*Applause.*)

JEAN

You don't tell me so. (*She turns the dials until she has picked up Rudy Vallee's band playing something or other.*) There—isn't that better? I'll tell you what, everybody. Let's roll back the carpets and have a little stepping, what do you say? Huh? (*There are a series of violent rings on the door-bell.*) Say! Maybe that's Harry now. I hope he left the storm upstairs. (*She goes to the hall door.*)

PHYLLIS

If it's Clarisse, you let me handle her. . . .

JEAN

Come on *in*, Harry, you big stupe!

MILT

Say—you're all *missing* it! It's right over the Sherry-Netherlands.

PHYLLIS

Now listen, Emma. You've got to go home!

JEAN (*horrified*)

My God! It's a raid! (*She retreats hastily. PETE, a detective, comes in, followed by CONWAY, a traffic officer.*)

PHYLLIS

What do *you* want?

PETE

Is Glassman here?

JEAN

No—he's upstairs. He lives in the penthouse. . . .

PETE

We've just been there and he ain't at home. Where is he?

PHYLLIS

Who are you?

(*An elevator boy, terribly scared, has come in in the wake of the cops.*)

PETE

I'm a policeman, madam.

PHYLLIS

In that case, probably you can tell me what business you've got coming into my apartment. . . .

PETE (*to the* ELEVATOR-MAN)

Who is this?

ELEVATOR-MAN

It's Miss Adrian. She's the tenant here.

PETE

Oh, Miss Phyllis Adrian. Quite a public character.

PHYLLIS

Have you got a warrant that lets you break into a private home?

PETE

No—I ain't got any warrant.

PHYLLIS

Then whistle for your blood-hounds and get out.

PETE

Kind of fresh, eh?

PHYLLIS

Yes, and what's more, I'll tell you something. You'd better be careful how you talk to me, because I happen to be a personal friend of the mayor of this city.

PETE

Well, who isn't? Where's Glassman?

PHYLLIS

How should I know?

PETE

That's your problem. But he ain't in his own place, and he ain't left this building—at least, so far as the operator knows. . . . We'd better take a look around, Con.

PATROLMAN

O. K. (*He starts toward the dining room.*)

PHYLLIS

He's in the bedroom.

PETE

In there?

PHYLLIS

Yes.

PETE

Bring him out, Con. (CONWAY *goes out at the left.* PETE *produces his note-book.*) Now—if no one objects, I might take a few names. (*He looks at* MILT.) Who are you?

MILT

John Smith.

PETE

No! Not *the* John Smith. (*He sees* BABE SA-VITO.) Hi, Babe.

BABE

Hi. (*The radio has been going all this time, the orchestral part having given way to Rudy's inevitable solo.*)

PETE

Now there's one guy I don't want to hear from is Rudy Vallee. . . . Turn that off. (*Someone turns it off.* GLASSMAN *comes in, followed by* CONWAY.) Good evening, Harry.

GLASSMAN

Good evening, Pete. What's the idea?

PETE

How long have you been down here?

GLASSMAN

I don't know.

PETE

You'd better know.

GLASSMAN

Fifteen or twenty minutes, I guess.

PETE

Can you prove that?

GLASSMAN

Prove what? What are you getting at, Pete?
What's wrong?

PETE

Your servants upstairs didn't see you leave the
apartment.

GLASSMAN

They weren't there. They were down here,
helping.

(*The* JUDGE *comes in with a highball.*)

JUDGE

Well, have you sweethearts settled your . . .

PETE

Hi, Judge.

JUDGE

Say! What's coming off here?

GLASSMAN

Miss Peretti was up there. She saw me go.
She'll tell you.

PETE

Miss Peretti ain't telling. And she ain't going to.

GLASSMAN (*scared*)

What's the matter with her?

PETE

She's dead.

PHYLLIS

Oh!

(PATROLMAN KAVANAUGH, *a thin cop, ambles in.*)

JUDGE

You mean she's dead?

GLASSMAN

She killed herself. . . .

PETE (*looking at his watch*)

A little over ten minutes ago she hit the pavement, on Eighth Avenue, after having fallen twenty-one stories. . . .

GLASSMAN

Don't tell me about it. I don't want to hear it.

JUDGE

Take it easy, Harry. (*To* PETE.) Well—what of it?

PETE

This officer and I saw her land. The doorman identified her, and we went up to apartment 21-B. There were signs of a struggle all over the place. . . .

GLASSMAN

She was crazy, Pete. She's been feeling bad for months. You can't blame her for doing a thing like that when she was crazy.

Pete

I said—there were signs of a struggle, especially right around the only window in the apartment that was open. It looked a lot to me as if the girl had been fighting for her life.

(*Another patrolman,* Sztineck, *comes in.*)

Glassman (*approaching* Pete)

What are you saying? Are you trying to tell me that I could do a thing like . . .?

Judge

I'll be going. . . .

Glassman

And leave me to get myself out of this the best way I . . .

Judge

What's the matter with *you?* Have the guts fallen down on you? (*He turns to* Pete.) Now, ask plenty of questions—and take your time about it. Do you get me?

Pete

O. K., Judge. (*The* Judge *goes.*)

Glassman

Go ahead. Get out of it, you yellow son of . . .

Phyllis

Keep quiet, Harry. He knows what he's doing. (*To* Pete.) There was a party going on upstairs, and then it moved down here. Everybody in this room can tell you everything that happened up to the time Clarisse was left alone, which she wanted to be. . . .

PETE (*to the* ELEVATOR-MAN)

Did you bring any of these people down in the car?

ELEVATOR-MAN

Well—first I brought Babe Savito, and that lady over there. Then there was another ring, and I brought him, and her and the judge (*indicating* MILT *and* SHEILA), and a couple of others that didn't get off here.

PETE

Was Glassman with them?

ELEVATOR-MAN

No, sir. I didn't see him.

PETE

How'd you get down, Harry?

GLASSMAN

I walked down.

JEAN

It's only two flights.

PETE (*to* JEAN)

Were you here when he came in?

JEAN

Well, I—I wasn't exactly in this room.

PETE

Where were you?

JEAN

In the dining room, having a little supper.

PETE

How about you, Babe?

BABE

I was in there, too. And the door was closed. Somebody shut it.

PETE

Anybody else with you?

JEAN (*indicating* SHEILA)

This lady was with us, and so was the judge.

MILT

And so was I.

JEAN

We didn't have the faintest idea of what was going on.

PETE (*to* GLASSMAN)

Well! It looks like everybody was somewhere else at the crucial moment.

PHYLLIS

I was here, you fat-head. I had a long talk with him.

PETE

You were the only one?

EMMA

No—I was . . .

PHYLLIS

You keep out of this. You're not needed.

PETE

What were you saying?

EMMA

I was here all through it. It was easily twenty minutes ago when this gentleman came in.

PETE

Who are you?

PHYLLIS

Her name's Jessup.

PETE

What?

EMMA

Jessup—Florence Jessup. . . .

PETE

Where do you live?

PHYLLIS

She comes from out West. She's just here on a visit.

PETE

Seeing the sights, I suppose. (*He glances around at the assemblage.*) Well, Harry—you've got two nice alibis. But we'll have to wait and see just how much they're good for. In the meantime, I think we'd all better take a little taxi ride over to West 68th Street and talk things over. . . . Want to get your coat and hat?

GLASSMAN

Yes. They're upstairs.

PETE

Go with him, Con. I'll be up in a minute.

GLASSMAN (*at the door*)

Say, Pete. . . . She—she isn't up there . . .?

PETE

No.

(*As* GLASSMAN *is going out with* CONWAY, JOE *comes in—startled, of course, at the array of blue uniforms.*)

PETE

Who's this? You're a little late for the party.

JOE

What's happened? Who was it that they were . . . (*He makes a sort of gesture toward the street below.*)

PHYLLIS

It was Clarisse.

JOE

From here?

PHYLLIS

No—from her place.

JOE (*seeing* EMMA)

Emmy! What in the name of God are you doing here?

EMMA

I'm sorry, Joe.

PETE

Emmy! (*He looks at his note-book.*) Is that
short for Florence?

JOE (*to* PETE)

She hasn't got anything to do with this. She
doesn't know any of these people.

EMMA

I have to tell him, Joe. I was here.

(*Two* REPORTERS *rush in, one of them with a
camera.*)

CAMERA-MAN

Hello, Pete—can we get any pictures?

REPORTER (*looking around*)

My God, Ben—look who's all here. It's an
orgy.

PETE

Keep 'em quiet, Kav.

KAVANAUGH

Come on, boys—you'll have to wait.

BABE (*ferocious*)

You ain't got no excuse to get me into this. . . .

PETE

Don't get excited, Babe. Now, before we break up this party, I'd like to get things a little straighter. Will all of you kindly line up over there?

PHYLLIS

You needn't think you're kidding anybody with all this. (*She crosses to join the frightened group before the window.*)

JOE

She doesn't know a damned thing about this. You don't have to . . .

PETE

Get over there.

JOE

Look here, officer—(*he speaks to* PETE *in an undertone*)—my name is Gresham, and I'll be glad to fix this up . . .

PETE

You needn't bother about me. I'm not important enough to be bribed. Get over there.

EMMA

It's no use, Joe. I've got to do it. (*She goes over to join the line.* JOE *reluctantly follows.*)

PETE

Now—we're going to take down all the names —and this time, we're going to have only the *right* names. Who are you?

MILT

Milton M. Fliesler.

PETE

Address?

MILT

830 University Heights. I go to N. Y. U. I live with my mother.

PETE

That's great. . . . And you?

SHEILA

Sheila Lavery—Hotel Belgrave—Madison Avenue at 76th Street.

PETE

And you?

JEAN

Jean Doran, 365 East 49th Street. (*She has been sobbing softly. Now she bursts into hysterical laughter.*)

PETE

Ah—shut her up! . . . And Babe Savito.
. . . And how about you, Miss Jessup? What's
your name?

JOE

Don't tell him.

PHYLLIS

She gave her right name the first time.

PETE

Just repeat it—because I want to be sure to
have it straight when they call you for the Homicide Bureau.

EMMA

It's Emma Krull—Sioux Falls, South Dakota.
(*The* CAMERA-MAN *has been furtively focus-
sing his camera. There is a sudden flash-light ex-
plosion.*)

PETE

What the hell! I thought I told you guys . . .

REPORTER

It's all right, Pete. Just a little group.

PETE (*again to* EMMA)

How do you spell that last name?

EMMA

K-R-U-L-L.

JOE

Oh—God—almighty! (*It's a species of moan.*
EMMA *pats his hand, which is on her shoulder.*)

CURTAIN

ACT III

ACT III

SCENE: *The same as Act II, an hour or so later.*

There are some half-empty glasses about, and many teeming ash-trays.

LUCILLE is cleaning up the mess in a rather desultory manner, dumping the ash-trays on to a large tray which she carries.

PATROLMAN KAVANAUGH is listening to the radio, his ear close to the loud speaker, from which is issuing a virtually inaudible murmur. He is solemnly eating a sandwich.

LUCILLE makes something of a clatter with her work.

KAVANAUGH

Keep quiet! (LUCILLE *suspends her operations for the moment.*) Yeh—I was right. It's KMOX, St. Louis.

LUCILLE (*resuming*)

That's nothin'. We get Denver any time we want it.

(*The telephone rings. LUCILLE puts down her tray and starts toward it.*)

KAVANAUGH

I'll take that. . . . (*He goes to the telephone.*) . . . Yeh. . . . Who? . . . No—there's nobody here just now. . . . All right. . . . Who? . . . Senator who? . . . Is that a State senator, or one of the other ones? . . . Yeh. . . . Yeh. . . . O. K. . . . I'll tell her. . . . (*He hangs up.*)

LUCILLE

Was that the Senator wanting his daughter?

KAVANAUGH

Nah—it was some newspaper man. (*He takes a sandwich from the platter, which is still on the table, and bites into it.*) These sandwiches is stale.

LUCILLE

Had I better send out to Reuben's?

KAVANAUGH (*back at the radio*)

Hey—listen! They're playing "Little White Lies." (*He starts to dance with an imaginary partner.*)

LUCILLE

They play it better in Denver.

(*The front door is heard to open, and* PHYLLIS *comes in, followed by* EMMA, JOE *and* PATROL-MAN SZTINECK. PHYLLIS *goes to the radio and turns it off.*)

SZTINECK

Hi, Kav.

KAVANAUGH

Hi, Stink.

LUCILLE

Where'd they take you to, Miss Phil?

PHYLLIS

To the station house. We registered on the blotter.

KAVANAUGH

Is one of you Miss Krull?

EMMA

Yes—I am.

(LUCILLE *goes out with the tray, on which she has placed the mess.* JOE *has sat down on the couch, his hat still on. He is not cheerful.*)

KAVANAUGH

Well—some guy named Hauser from *The Telegram* called up to say he located your father.

EMMA

Where—at the hotel?

KAVANAUGH

Nah—he's been over to the station house, too, with your mother. Only they got into the wrong one, West 47th Street.

EMMA

Poor pop! Does he know where I am?

KAVANAUGH

That *Telegram* guy said to tell you he'd keep in touch.

EMMA

Thanks.

PHYLLIS

All I ask is you don't have the family reunion in here.

SZTINECK

You don't have to stick here any longer, Kav. The big chief's on the way. He's going to look it over upstairs, and then come down and ask you folks a few questions.

PHYLLIS

Tell him to make it fast, because we can't sit up all night.

KAVANAUGH

I'll see that he gets your message.

(SZTINECK *goes out.* KAVANAUGH *takes another sandwich and is about to follow him.*)

JOE

And tell those cops down in the lobby to shoot any newspaper men that try to get up here.

KAVANAUGH

I'd be glad to.

EMMA

Except that Mr. Hauser from *The Tele-gram*. . . .

PHYLLIS

Yes—we'll see him.

KAVANAUGH

O. K., ladies. (*He goes out.* EMMA *goes over to the mirror, at the left, to do some work on her appearance.*)

PHYLLIS

Don't you want to go into my room, Em, dar-ling?

EMMA

Thanks, I will. (*She goes out at the left, amaz-ingly unperturbed.*)

PHYLLIS (*to* JOE)

Take your hat off. (*He takes it off and throws it on the table.*) Do you want a drink?

JOE

Yes.

PHYLLIS

Lucille! (*To* JOE.) Scotch?

JOE

I think I'd rather have a cup of coffee.
(LUCILLE *comes in.*)

PHYLLIS

Bring a lot of coffee.

LUCILLE

And some scrambled eggs and bacon?

PHYLLIS

Want any eggs, Joe?

JOE

No!

PHYLLIS

Just the coffee, Lucille. (LUCILLE *goes*. PHYLLIS *looks at* JOE.) Now, listen—there's no excuse for you to sit there looking as if this was your private funeral. It's a tough break for everybody.

JOE

As though I give a damn what happens to Harry Glassman, or any of that outfit——

PHYLLIS

Well—I guess it hasn't been any fun for her, either. (*With a gesture toward the left.*) But have you heard her say one word of complaint? You have not.

JOE

Yes—*she* has some idea of what it is to be a good sport.

PHYLLIS

Just what you crave, isn't she?

JOE (*rising and pacing*)

Why did she come here?

PHYLLIS

Don't ask me.

JOE

I'm not asking you. I'm talking to myself.

PHYLLIS

Are you keeping yourself interested? (*The telephone rings.* PHYLLIS *answers it.*) Hello. . . . What? . . . Yes, certainly. You can get all the pictures of me you want in the art department of the Metropolitan Museum. . . . (*She hangs up.*) Listen, Joe—you're not going to take it out on her just because there was an accident. . . .

JOE

She was a crazy fool to step into this mess.

PHYLLIS

No, she wasn't. She was smart. She wanted to see something of the surroundings in which you grew up. . . . There aren't many girls, getting married, who have sense enough to study the technique of whoever it is they're following on the bill. . . .

JOE

I hope she learned a lot.

Phyllis

She'll always learn. And if it hadn't been for
. . . for what happened—I'll bet anything she'd
have done what she really came here for.

Joe

What?

Phyllis

To save you a lot of money. She'd have got me
to come down in my price. . . . I've got to hand
it to you, Joe. You certainly do pick clever
girls——

Joe

Yes—I run to the peaceful, homey type.

Phyllis

And I wouldn't be surprised if this last one
turned out to be the flower of the flock. . . . But
if you split up with her, I advise you next time to
get somebody *dumb*. You'll find it a lot safer.

(Emma *comes in.*)

Emma

How long do you suppose we'll have to wait?

Phyllis

There's no way of telling. The commissioner
is working on his own time.

Emma

He won't make any trouble, will he?

PHYLLIS

Oh—he'll make a big splurge, for the sake of publicity.

JOE

They haven't got any chance of proving it wasn't suicide.

PHYLLIS

No! But seeing it's a famous racketeer like Harry Glassman, the cops will play it up big. It'll help to take the public's mind away from all those vanishing judges.

EMMA

I feel terribly sorry for Mr. Glassman.

JOE

A worthy object of sympathy.

EMMA

Well, he really loved that girl.

PHYLLIS (*to* JOE)

And love is the most marvellous thing in the world, isn't it, sweets?

EMMA (*with a glance at* JOE)

It ought to be.

JOE

I'd be in more of a mood to talk about love if I could only stop thinking what the *Mirror, News* and *Graphic* will look like to-morrow.

EMMA

Do you suppose that girl had any family?

PHYLLIS

I don't know. I never even knew her right name.
She told me once she came from Little Rock.
Maybe she did. . . . But don't be thinking about
her, Em. She didn't have any notion of what was
happening. The condition she was in, I guess she
thought she was flying, out over the trees in the
park.

JOE

Like Peter Pan.

(*The telephone rings.* PHYLLIS *goes and answers it.*)

PHYLLIS

This line is busy! (*She leaves the telephone dis-
connected.*) What you want to do, both of you,
is learn the Broadway idea. When somebody dies,
or gets killed, just tell yourself, "Well—when all
is said and done, it's the best thing that could
have happened to poor So-and-so." That mayn't
be true, but it gives you a good excuse for for-
getting all about it. (*She looks at herself in the
mirror at the left, then goes into the bedroom.*)

EMMA

There's something I'd like to know, Joe.

JOE

Hasn't your desire for knowledge been satisfied
yet?

EMMA

Why—why did you come back here to-night?

JOE

Why indeed.

EMMA

Was it because you wanted to see Phil again?

JOE

Yes, it was . . . I came back here to tell her I'd got the money.

EMMA

All of it?

JOE

All of it. One hundred thousand dollars.

EMMA

Joe! How did you get it?

JOE

I went to my father. I faced it out with him. I promised him that if he'd advance me that much, in cash, I'd never get mixed up in any kind of scrape again. He said he'd heard that before. Then I told him that if he didn't come through, I'd do some things he *hadn't* heard of. I swore to him that I'd find ways and means to disgrace the whole family—aunts, cousins and all. And that scared him, because he knew damned well I was capable of doing it. . . . Well—I seem to have made a good start to-night. . . .

EMMA

That was brave of you, dear. . . .

JOE

My great bravery was wasted.

EMMA

No, it wasn't.

JOE

Everything that I've done has been wrong, from start to finish. Well—anyway—when you see your father you can have the satisfaction of telling him that you've learned your lesson, and that the engagement is off.

EMMA

Joe!

JOE

And you can tell him also that he's entirely right in his opinion of me and of this rotten city. The whole place is a nightmare.

EMMA

But we could live somewhere else, couldn't we?

JOE

You can live wherever you want to, but not with me.

EMMA

Why not?

JOE (*impatiently*)

Because I love you.

EMMA

Somehow or other, that doesn't seem to follow.

JOE

I love you so much that I couldn't bear to see
you condemned to spend your life with a weak, ineffectual, vicious imbecile like me.
(PHYLLIS *comes in.*)

PHYLLIS

Hasn't she cooked that coffee yet?

EMMA

Joe has some strange news for us, Phil.

PHYLLIS

What is it?

EMMA

He went to his father, and he collected that
hundred thousand dollars, to pay you off. Did
you ever hear of such heroism?

PHYLLIS

Why, Joe—I'm overcome!

JOE

It's some consolation to know that *you* won't
see a nickel of it.

EMMA

You're not going to pay her?

JOE

After what's happened? It's too late now for her to do any damage. That's been done. The beans have been spilled.

PHYLLIS

I'm afraid he's right, Em.

JOE

However—when you want any letters of recommendation to the boys at the Racquet Club, don't hesitate to call on me.

PHYLLIS

Just write me out a blanket endorsement—to whom it may concern.

EMMA

And what's more, Phil—he's broken off with me.

PHYLLIS

What!

EMMA

He's through with me.

PHYLLIS

Oh, he is, is he? Well, don't you fret about that, little girl. There's someone I want to put you in touch with. It's a Mr. Nicholas Pinanski, of Callahan, Pinan . . . (*The door-bell rings.*) See who that is, Lucille. Don't let 'em in. (*She goes to the hall entrance.*) Come on, now—get out of here. (*She has gone into the hall.*) We're not seeing any . . . What! (*She comes back into the room.*) She's in here.

(KRULL *and* MRS. KRULL *come in.*)

EMMA (*jumping up*)

Pop!

KRULL

We've been trying to find you for two hours. We were shocked, stunned. We didn't know where to turn, what to do. . . .

EMMA

I tried to reach you. I called the hotel, twice.

MRS. KRULL

Do you fully realize what it is you've *done?*

EMMA

It couldn't be helped, Mother. . . .

JOE

It was my fault, Mrs. Krull. Em was only trying to . . .

KRULL

Fault? Fault! What difference who's fault it was? All that matters is the shameful fact that my daughter . . .

EMMA

Now, *please*, Pop! Don't start it now, because I just can't . . .

(*Nobody is being allowed to finish a sentence in the intense agitation.*)

JOE

There's no reason for you to blame Em for anything. She . . .

MRS. KRULL (*too loud*)

We have no desire to hear *your* version of this!

EMMA

Mother! You won't help matters at all by shouting.

KRULL

Perhaps you'll help matters by giving us an immediate explanation of this horror.

EMMA

I will, Pop. I'll explain the whole thing. But not now.

PHYLLIS

Wouldn't you like to sit down, Mrs. Krull?

(*PHYLLIS has been remaining discreetly out of it, but she intrudes in a commendable attempt to do some soothing.*)

MRS. KRULL

Thank you, no!

Emma

This is Miss Adrian—my mother and father.

Phyllis

How do you do? I *wish* you'd sit down. You must be terribly tired.

Krull

We've come to take our daughter back to the hotel. Are you ready to go, Emma?

Emma

I can't leave here yet, Pop.

Mrs. Krull

Are you still in custody?

Emma

They told us to wait.

Joe

The Police Commissioner is coming to ask questions.

Krull

And when will he be here?

Phyllis

We haven't heard.

Mrs. Krull

And to-morrow I was to have joined my colleagues of the Daughters of the American Revolution!

EMMA

You don't need to wait here now, Mother. The Commissioner doesn't want to see you.

MRS. KRULL

We will wait!

KRULL

You broke your word of honor to your mother and me.

EMMA

I did not.

MRS. KRULL

You promised faithfully that you wouldn't see him again this evening. (*This is indicating* JOE.)

JOE

She didn't, Mrs. Krull. I swear it was entirely . . .

MRS. KRULL (*scornfully*)

I have said that we do not . . .

EMMA

I came here by myself. Joe didn't know anything about it.

JOE

If you'd only let me stay there, to watch her, she wouldn't have stirred out of the hotel.

KRULL

I suppose you're aware that this sickening affair is going to get into the papers.

JOE

Yes—we've had some hints of that.

MRS. KRULL

Ever since we heard about it we've been assailed by . . .

EMMA

When did you hear?

MRS. KRULL

Your father had barely completed his address —when the reporters appeared. They crawled over us like vermin, shouting that our child had been implicated in a murder, with a beer baron, and a prize-fighter, in a love nest!

JOE

It wasn't a murder. It was suicide.

KRULL

And don't think it's limited to the New York papers. Among the hooligans who have been following me about this city was a representative of the Associated Press. All the gruesome revelations are being flashed throughout the length and breadth of the United States. Unfortunately, your participation gives this tragedy a national significance.

(LUCILLE *comes in with a tray on which are a silver coffee pot and three large cups.*)

PHYLLIS

Ah! Here's the coffee. Just what we all need.
. . . Mrs. Krull, won't you have some?

MRS. KRULL (*shortly*)

I don't think so.

PHYLLIS

Senator? (*She is pouring the coffee.*)

KRULL

No! I don't want any coffee!

JOE

Neither do I, now.

PHYLLIS

Take it away, Lucille.

LUCILLE

Yes, Miss Phil. (*She goes.*)

JOE

I know perfectly well that you hold me respon-
sible for all of this. And you're not doing me any
injustice if you do.

KRULL

We're aware of that.

MRS. KRULL

I think you can save yourself the effort of trying to make any explanations, young man.

PHYLLIS (*to* MRS. KRULL)

When the whole story comes out, as it certainly will, you'll find out that it's really my fault that Em got mixed up in all this. You see, Mrs. Krull, the trouble with me is I'm just the least bit mercenary. . . .

KRULL

May I ask you who you are, and just why my daughter saw fit to enter your . . .

JOE

I'll tell you who she is, Senator. She's my—she was my mistress. She was blackmailing me.

PHYLLIS

That about sums me up.

EMMA

And I stepped in and fixed everything.
(*The door-bell rings.*)

MRS. KRULL

I don't care to stay here, Harvey. . . .

LUCILLE (*coming in*)

It's that reporter—the one you said was O. K.

PHYLLIS

All right. Let him in.

KRULL

Do we have to have a reporter?

EMMA

I sent for him, Pop. He's the one from *The
Telegram*. He's helping us.

(HAUSER *comes in*.)

HAUSER (*surprised to encounter* KRULL)

Oh! Good evening, Senator . . . I'm very
sorry that we should meet again under such unfortunate . . .

KRULL

The situation calls for no comment.

JOE (*muttering*)

If that were only true!

EMMA

What have you heard?

HAUSER

I've been down at headquarters, and I think I
can assure you that everything is going to be all
right.

MRS. KRULL

They're going to suppress this whole scandal-
ous story?

HAUSER

I'm afraid they can hardly do that. But they'll
bring in a verdict of suicide, sure. The authorities
can't touch Harry Glassman, and they know it.
. . . However—the papers are bound to make a
lot of noise about it, because of Glassman's no-

toriety. So the police want to make a great show of investigating the matter thoroughly before they slap on the white-wash. That's why the commissioner is taking a personal hand. It makes it look as if he meant business. (*This last is in the nature of an explanation to the senator.*)

KRULL

And when Tammany Hall has completed this— this mock display—will my daughter be called upon for any further participation?

HAUSER

There'll be the Homicide Bureau investigation, of course—a routine formality. It would look a little strange if Miss Krull avoided that. She's the only really respectable alibi that Glassman has got.

PHYLLIS

I love that!

HAUSER

I don't suppose, Senator, you could be induced to issue a statement on this regrettable occurrence?

KRULL

I don't suppose I could.

HAUSER

If I might offer a suggestion, Senator—it might look well if you were to say something in—in extenuation of your daughter's part in this. . . .

KRULL

Are you daring to suggest that Miss Krull requires any exten . . .?

HAUSER

Oh, no, no—I was only considering the possible effect on public opinion, especially out in your own section of the . . .

EMMA

He has the right idea, Pop. Remember what Heflin did.

MRS. KRULL

All things considered, I believe you should announce that in so far as we are concerned, no disgrace whatever attaches to Emma's name.

KRULL

Very well. You can quote me as saying that Mrs. Krull and I are standing squarely behind our daughter in this emergency. (*Almost unconsciously, he takes on the manner of one who is dictating an important letter, choosing his words.*) We are aware of all the circumstances surrounding her—her involvement, and we are thoroughly satisfied that they reflect no discredit whatever on her character. . . .

MRS. KRULL

Senator Krull is first, last and always a loving father, and I am a mother!

HAUSER

That's perfect! (*He jots down the words "mother gag" on a wad of copy paper which he has taken from his pocket.*)

KRULL

You'll see to it that that statement goes to the press *outside* New York?

HAUSER

Oh, yes, Senator. The U. P. will send it out everywhere.

KRULL

And you might add that this sordid affair only tends to confirm my previous opinions of the conditions of civilization in New York City. It's a sewer!

PHYLLIS

The Chicago papers will certainly print that.

HAUSER

Thank you very much, Senator. I'll be running along now—unless there's anything more that I can do. . . .

EMMA

Thanks. You've been fine.

HAUSER

It's been a pleasure.

JOE (*with a look*)

Hasn't it!

HAUSER

Well—good night, everybody. (*He goes out.*)

MRS. KRULL (*to* EMMA)

Do you see now what you've subjected us to? The Homicide Bureau!

EMMA

Oh, I'm sorry, Mother. I've done an awful thing to you and Pop. And I won't blame you if you disown me, cast me out. . . .

KRULL

We contemplate no such course of action. We're going to take you home, to Sioux Falls, and we'll face it out together—even if it costs me the election. . . .

EMMA

It couldn't do that. You'll be more popular than ever when the people of South Dakota see what a fine, loyal, devoted father you are.

MRS. KRULL

It's a relief to know that you've discovered some good in your parents, after all these years.

KRULL

My dear child—I've never had the slightest doubt in my mind that you'd work out your destiny in the right way. I know you're head-strong, and independent—but you come by it honestly. It's the pioneer blood that flows through your veins. But now you've witnessed a typical demonstration of their vaunted Eastern culture.

JOE

You call this typical?

KRULL

I do! Every phase of it! And particularly the twenty-story leap to death. And I thank God that, horrible as it is, it has given my daughter vision to see the truth. (*He addresses* EMMA.) After you've been home a while, and got yourself back to normal, you'll appreciate what an escape you've had. (KRULL *is becoming increasingly pleased with the trend of the conversation. He considers that he is scoring some telling points.*) And one of these days you'll find some clean-limbed young American *man*, and you'll marry him, as the good Lord meant you to.

PHYLLIS

And raise a whole brood of candidates for the U. S. Senate.

(JOE *comes down from the aloof position he had been occupying, upstage.*)

JOE

Are you going to do that, Em?

Mrs. Krull

She is! (*She turns to* Krull.) I approve everything you've said, Harvey. You're a good, Christian gentleman.

Joe

Em! Are you going to do what your father says?

Emma

You *are* a Christian gentleman, Pop. You could have raved and ranted at me, and thrown me out onto the streets. Or worse, you could have said that you forgive me. But you haven't, and I'm grateful to you, and I'll always be grateful. . . . But I've said that I was going to be married to Joe, and I intend to do it . . . even in spite of the fact that he doesn't approve of the match.

Mrs. Krull

You propose to complete the disgrace that you've started this night?

Emma

It isn't a disgrace, Mother. You said so yourself, to that reporter.

Krull

You mean that, my daughter? You mean that knowing what you do of his character, seeing what you have seen of his environment, you still refuse to give him up?

EMMA

Yes, Pop. I mean it.

(JOE *seizes her hand and holds it tightly.*)

PHYLLIS

She does, Senator. It's that old pioneer blood.

MRS. KRULL (*to* KRULL)

You can't stand by and let this happen. You can force her to obey you, to do what you know is right.

JOE

You can't force her. God only knows why she's made this choice, but she's made it.

KRULL (*very tense*)

You're quite right. I can't do it. It's too late for that. We've got to face the bitter fact of our own failure to hold the child that we bred. We haven't disowned her—but she has renounced us, and everything that we stand for. She has chosen to become an alien. So be it! I will make no further attempt to reclaim her. Let her rot in the charnel-house that she has selected as her habitation. . . . Come—we'd better be going on. . . .

JOE

Just a minute, Senator. I've made every conceivable effort to ingratiate myself, and avoid any open conflict with you. I don't seem to have been very successful. So I'll stop being discreet just long enough to tell you that I think you damned well ought to be ashamed of yourself for talking that way to your daughter!

EMMA

You can't say that, Joe, because you don't understand what's behind my father. . . .

JOE

I understand that statement that you gave out to the press. Loyalty, devotion! If you'll forgive me for saying so—it's bunk! All you thought about was making a good impression on your constituents. You'll stand up for Em, yes—just as long as she conforms to your South Dakota ideas of morality, just as long as she lives the kind of narrow life that . . .

EMMA

Joe! You've got to stop that! Don't listen to him, Pop. He isn't being . . .

KRULL

I am listening to him. I'm treasuring every word he says. I am glorying in the realization that such as he is opposed in every way to such as I—the realization that I have been right, eternally right, when I have said that New York is not America. . . .

PHYLLIS

Now listen . . .

JOE

You keep your mouth shut.

PHYLLIS

I've heard that crack before. Will Rogers always gets a hand with it when he's playing Chautauqua time. Well—what I want to know is, if you foreigners don't like it here, why don't you go back where you came from—and take your amendments with you?

KRULL

It's peculiarly appropriate that the spirit of this city should find voice in one of your kind.

MRS. KRULL

You're degrading yourself by entering into any discussion with her.

PHYLLIS

Why don't you get into it yourself, Mrs. Krull? It's turning into a free-for-all.

KRULL

By God—I wish the whole pack of you *would* secede, and precipitate another Civil War, so that the true patriots might have an opportunity to wipe out this—this bawdy shambles of law-breakers, and millionaire wastrels, and drug addicts, and perverts and harlots. . . .

EMMA

That's right, Pop. Stand up to 'em.

JOE (*to* KRULL)

I suppose there aren't any law-breakers or harlots in Sioux Falls. . . .

KRULL

If there are, it's because this city with its stinking money power is seducing the inherently decent minds of our people. . . .

PHYLLIS

I thought it was Hollywood that was supposed to be doing that.

KRULL

Hollywood is the illegitimate offspring of Broadway!

PHYLLIS

Don't let Will Hays hear that.

KRULL

Oh—you New Yorkers are willing enough to exploit America, to suck America's life-blood— and at the same time to champion every cause that's un-American, to flout the Constitution, to sneer at the very flag itself!

JOE

Oh, for God's sake! Who cares what's un-American and what isn't?

KRULL

Who, indeed, in this European pig-sty!

EMMA

Don't argue, Joe. You're not in Pop's class as a debater.

JOE

I don't want to argue. (*He approaches the senator.*) I only want to agree with you, Senator, and be on your side, and admit that the whole thing is rotten, and degraded.

KRULL

I do not solicit your support.

JOE

You believe that I'm speaking in good faith, don't you, Mrs. Krull?

MRS. KRULL

I do not! You'd best leave your defense to this trollop of yours.

EMMA

Mother!

PHYLLIS

That's what I am, Mrs. Krull. A hundred per cent American trollop!

KRULL

Don't you befoul the name of my country by mentioning it in that . . .

PHYLLIS

Your country! Your exclusive country? Would you like to know where I come from, Senator? I come from Texas. That's in America, too.

KRULL

I take note that you've found your own level, here.

PHYLLIS

I got here just the same way that you got to Washington. You're not the only one who has represented the U. S. in an official way. You may not know it, but I've been Miss America in my time. Yes, sir! I carried the Stars and Stripes in the International Beauty Contest, and what's more, I won. If it hadn't been for me, the championship would have gone to Czecho-Slovakia. And then where would our great nation have been? So maybe you'll pay a little more attention to me when I tell you that New York *is* America—boot-leggers and millionaires and crooked politicians and all. In fact—that's my chief complaint against this town.

EMMA

That's enough, Phil. It's a dirty, low trick to

pick on my father. You can get him at a disad-
vantage—because he needs votes, and you don't.

Mrs. Krull (*to* Krull)

Will you please take me away from this place
at once?

Emma

No! You've got to listen to *me*, both of you!

Mrs. Krull (*almost tearful*)

We've heard about enough of cynical irrever-
ence. We've suffered enough humiliation.

Krull

What have you got to say?

Emma

Just that I'm not planning to renounce you or
mother or our native land or Joe, either. He and
I are going to be married, right away, and as soon
as we've attended to that, we're going to move
out to Sioux Falls, South Dakota. And when
we get there, you're going to buy a ranch (*this to*
Joe)—thousands and thousands of acres—
thereby relieving a lot of starving farmers that
aren't any too grateful to you, Pop, for what
you haven't done for them. And Joe is going to
give out statements to all the local papers, pan-
ning New York and explaining that he's come out
to the Great West to live, and breathe fresh air,

and cleanse his system of the poison of the Big Evil City. And he'll become a popular hero over night with all the women voters—your buddies, Mother—because there's nothing they love so much as a New Yorker who has reformed. Joe, you'll be adopted as a prodigal son of the prairies. You'll wear a ten-gallon hat and make speeches. And you'll contribute handsomely to Pop's campaign fund. Why—for the price of one of your race horses you could buy all the votes there *are* in South Dakota. And on November the fourth Senator Krull and the Republican party will ride in to victory on an overwhelming wave of public enthusiasm. . . . (*She turns again to* JOE.) And when Election Day is over, you and I will move back and live on East 72d Street.

PHYLLIS

You can't beat that, Senator. She's got you licked—and on your own home grounds, too. You're not the last politician in the Krull family.

EMMA

And you needn't think he's going to let you down, Phil. He can easily spare, say, twenty-five thousand dollars.

JOE

What?

PHYLLIS

You mean I'm to split with the Senator?

EMMA

I think that's only fair.
(*The door-bell rings.*)

PHYLLIS

Twenty-five grand! With that I could get myself a coat of Riviera tan and come home a practically new woman, all set to go back into circulation. (*Looking out into the hall.*) Hello, Harry. (GLASSMAN *comes in.*) Is everything all right, Harry?

JUDGE (*coming in briskly*)

Everything's lovely! Old Harry thought I was walking out on him. As if I'd two-time a pal! I was just in a hurry to get things fixed, and when I say fixed, I mean . . . (*He sees* KRULL.) Well! Senator Krull, I believe. I'm glad to know you, Senator. I'm Judge Gohagan. (*He has extended his hand.*)

KRULL

Good evening.

JUDGE

Great little girl you've got there, Senator. Full of the right stuff. I regret she must be detained for questioning, but you'll appreciate that our police force must be on the alert.

KRULL

We know all about that!

GLASSMAN (*to* EMMA)

I want to thank you for the way you came across for me. It was God-damned decent of you to . . .

EMMA (*hastily*)

Oh, that's perfectly all right, Mr. Glassman.

JUDGE

As a matter of fact, Senator, there was no real need for your daughter to be dragged into this. I mean to say, if they'd only had sense enough to leave the works to me. . . .

KRULL

My daughter can stand on her own two feet, thank you!

JUDGE

Certainly she can. But just the same, a word or two in the right place sometimes saves a lot of trouble—but I guess I don't have to tell you anything about that, huh? (*Very knowing.*)

GLASSMAN (*still to* EMMA)

Maybe I'll be able to do something for you, some time.

PHYLLIS

You can do something for her, Harry. You can help her father get re-elected to the Senate. (GLASSMAN *has a good luck at* KRULL. *Then he turns to* EMMA.)

GLASSMAN

Don't you worry about that, kid. He's in now.

(*A* CAMERA-MAN *comes in, bearing his camera with tripod, and saying, "Here comes the commissioner!" On his heels comes another* CAMERA-MAN, *also saying, "Here comes the commissioner!" They set up their cameras.* PATROLMEN KAVANAUGH *and* SZTINECK *appear and stand at attention.*)

PHYLLIS (*going to the door*)

Oh! Come right in, Commissioner.

CURTAIN

410